Something of the Wonderful

by
John M. Scott, S.J.

ST. PAUL EDITIONS

NIHIL OBSTAT:
    Rev. Richard V. Lawlor, S.J.
    Censor

IMPRIMATUR:
    ✠ Bernard Cardinal Law, D.D.
    Archbishop of Boston

*   Permission for use granted by Loyola University Press
** Permission granted for use
*** Permission given for use granted by Sunshine magazine

Library of Congress Cataloging in Publication Data

Scott, John Martin, 1913-
    Something of the wonderful.

    1. Youth—Conduct of life. 2. Biography.
I. Title.
BJ1661.S355   1985   920'.02 [B]   85-13139

ISBN 0-8198-6867-1 c
    0-8198-6868-X p

Printed in the U.S.A., by the Daughters of St. Paul
50 St. Paul's Ave., Boston, MA 02130

The Daughters of St. Paul are an international congregation of women religious serving the Church with the communications media.

CONTENTS

Dedicated to
the memory of

BING CROSBY

who brought joy
and inspiration
to us all.

Introduction

Even though Ma Bell has not yet invented a telephone that will leap across the black holes of space and soar beyond the gleaming galaxies of far-distant stars, the truth is that we can dial ourselves into instant contact with friends and loved ones, long gone, but never forgotten.

At any moment of the day or night, we may make personal contact with wonderful people who once walked on planet earth with God by their side, and who may now be living with Him in joy.

How marvelous to realize that we may actually contact and speak to the best and most wonderful people of all times. The fact that they may have lived centuries before us means nothing.

The invitation extended to you in this book is well phrased by a bumper sticker on a car, "You Are a Child of God. Please Call Home."

A number of years ago when Pope John Paul II was known as Karol Wojtyla, Archbishop of Krakow, he wrote a number of poems. In one of his finest poems he said, "I am a giver, I touch forces that expand the mind."

My aim in this book is the same, to "touch forces that expand the mind" and let you experience something of the wonderful, unseen world that surrounds us on all sides.

This book will help you break the surly bonds of earth, to leap where stars are strewn, to pace the cold, black desert dunes of space, meander past whirling suns, until you orbit the rim of heaven itself. Your discoveries will make your heart beat fast with wonder, and your spirit shout with joy.

An Incredible

Invitation to You!

The person responsible for this book is the late and deeply-loved Pope John Paul I, the "September Pope."

Since Pope John Paul I reigned only 34 days, and did not have time to write even one major document, how can he be blamed for the title of this book?

The answer goes back to the early 1970's when Albino Luciani was the patriarch of Venice, and wrote a column for the Italian devotional magazine, the *Messenger of St. Anthony*. His contributions took the form of many whimsical "letters" to past personalities. In 1976 these "letters" were collected in a book put out by the St. Anthony Messenger Press called *Illustrissimi* (Most Illustrious People).

Among his many fictional correspondents was Sir Walter Scott. "Honor to the Scotsman and the creator of the clean historical novel. I repeat it sincerely, though I have small reservations about the arrows shot here and there against the Catholic Church."

Cardinal Luciani went on to extol the "courage and loyalty" in Scott's novels and expresses "astonish-

3

ment that despite today's deluge of morally degrading literature, young people are still drawn to them."

In a letter he wrote to Charles Dickens, the late Pope informed the famous English author that he liked his novels as a boy because "they are imbued with a sense of love for the poor and of social regeneration, and are rich with fantasy and humanity."

In his letter to Mark Twain, Albino Luciani admitted he was aware that some people would criticize him for picking Twain for a pen pal, but this did not discourage the future Pope. He admitted that some bishops are so gifted that they are like eagles cruising through the sky with dazzling documents. Some are like nightingales who marvelously sing the praises of the Lord. Others, instead, are only poor wrens, who can only twitter to express a few thoughts on sublime subjects. "I, dear Twain," said the future Pope, "belong to the latter category."

In his letter to Jesus, the Cardinal admitted that he had come under fire from many sides. "He is a Cardinal," people have said. "He has been busy writing letters in all directions. To Mark Twain, to Peguy and who knows to how many others. And not even one line to Jesus Christ."

In his defense the Cardinal wrote to Jesus, "But You know that I try to maintain a continuous conversation with You."

The few samples from Pope John Paul's letters will show why he is spoken of as "a whimsical scholar with a gift for words." He had a sense of humor, and a wide range of cultural interests.

After reading some of Pope John Paul's "letters," the thought jumped into my cranium, "Instead of writ ing 'letters' to illustrious people of the past, I'll call them up long distance and speak to them in person."

"Incredible," you retort. "You must be the fellow who flew over the cuckoo's nest. How under the seven stars of the Big Dipper can you talk with someone who no longer dwells on the planet earth?"

At any moment of the day or night, we may make personal contact with wonderful people who once walked on planet earth with God by their side, and who now may be living with Him in joy.

The way of making contact with people in heaven is known as prayer!

Prayer has been defined as "lifting up the mind and heart to God and/or His saints."

The canonized saints are those who have received official recognition from the Church. Their names are published in the official list of saints' names.

In addition to those who get "Official Listing" in the "Yellow Pages" or index of your prayer book, there are the saints with "silent numbers." Their names are not emblazoned in stained glass windows, nor do they appear in the mastheads of church bulletins. The un-canonized saints are those friends of God who now dwell in the joy and beauty of our Father's house. They enjoy the happiness of heaven where God wipes away all tears from our eyes, and death shall be no more.

The galaxy of saints for you to choose from is as numerous as the twinkling stars that oversprinkle a midsummer's night.

To have the saints for friends, you don't have to pay union dues, belong to the Elks Club, or win the

Nobel Prize. Just spin your prayer dial to H-E-A-V-E-N and establish direct contact with the most fascinating men and women of all times.

Your favorite saint may be someone from your own family, someone very near and dear to you. If they loved you when they walked this earth, they love you now a thousandfold more. Their love is forever yours. Each day they follow your tribulations and trials with sympathy and prayers.

Down the days and down the nights and down the long avenues of the years their love is a star from heaven that points the way, and leads us to our home.

"Surely it is a wonderful favor," says Father T. N. Jorgensen, S.J., "to be invited to live with the most wonderful people of all times. And we are invited to do just that. To live with them, to talk to them, to love them and to be one with them. Their love is ours to enjoy. Their presence is ours to rejoice in, if we but wish.

"The spiritual life is not hard or sad or unnatural. God wishes us to love the good, the joyous, and the beautiful things of time and eternity."

Devotion to the saints conquers loneliness, confusion and despair by bringing us companionship, peace, joy, hope and inspiration to help us carry on amid the sufferings and hardships of life.

Thanks to the Communion of Saints, we have friends to walk by our side always.

When night approaches on soft and beautiful feet, coming first gently and slowly from afar, then swiftly, and with her mantle of silence and darkness covering all things, look up into the galaxy of stars, white and topaz and misty red—myriads with beating hearts of fire that eons cannot quench or tire.

As you look, you can almost hear the whispers of your dreams. You put your hand into the hand of the one you love, and walk down that gleaming highway in the sky, the Milky Way.

In this age of built-up vitamin pills, smashed atoms and space shuttle orbiters, people like to find their name in *Who's Who*, to see their picture on the society page, and to hear their names coming from the radio. But why envy them?

We, as members of the Communion of Saints, daily rub shoulders with the greatest men and women in history. We can have for our friends the most wonderful, the most exciting, the most inspirational people of all times.

Some people think the Golden Age will dawn when they have April in Paris, the surf at Oahu, the conquest of Everest, the Bermuda Race, a creel of rainbow trout, Derby Day at Epsom Downs; Acapulco, Malibu, Yankee Stadium, and Bonneville Flats.

Yet the Golden Age surrounds you whether you live on the west end of Butte, Montana, in a bungalow built for two, or in the Chicago Hilton.

The Golden Age here and now offers you the opportunity to have for your companions the most fascinating men and women of history; to be friends with the most charming women and captivating men ever to breathe the ozone of planet earth.

The whole world is God's. We are all His children. How marvelous to realize that we may actually contact and speak to the best and most wonderful people of all times. The fact that the saints may have lived centuries before us means nothing. We can contact them this moment in prayer.

Listen to the inspiring words of Cardinal Manning, "Let us learn that we can never be lonely or forsaken in this life. Shall they forget us because they are made perfect? Shall they love us less because they now have the power to love us more? The heavenly world hangs serenely overhead; only a thin veil floats between. All whom we loved and all who loved us are ever near."

When I was in Ireland I discovered that the people talked about God and the saints as easily as they did about their friends; and they took it for granted that you, too, were on such familiar terms with the saints and God.

No wonder that H.V. Morton wrote of the Irish, "They live in the shadow of God. They talk about Him as though He helped them that morning to bake the soda-bread in the peat-embers."

What an incredible invitation is yours! It makes no difference whether you are a patient in room 364 of the Bergan Mercy Hospital in Omaha, Nebraska, or whether you are peeling potatoes in your kitchen in Silverton, Oregon; you have a most unique privilege. You have an invitation to claim for your personal friends the most lovely and fascinating people of all time.

You may not have a big bank account in the First National. You may not have a $150,000.00 home on the west end of town. Your name may not appear in the society section of the *Chicago Tribune* or the *Denver Post;* nevertheless you are important. You are a child of God. Heaven is your home, and through the miracle of prayer you may contact all who have gone before us into the joy of the Lord.

When you look through your window at night, how thrilling and satisfying to look up at the gleaming stars and catch, as it were, the reflection of the smiles of those you love. Better still to realize that your loved ones stand unseen by your side. Their love—pure as a pearl and warm as a ruby—is yours to enjoy forever.

You need never feel alone with the beating of your heart. Just as certainly as there is oxygen in the air we breathe (even though unseen and not detected by our senses), so, too, is the continued presence of our loved ones.

That it is an unseen presence does not make it less valuable. And their help is nonetheless powerful because it is unseen by physical eyes. (The oxygen we breathe is nonetheless powerful because it is unseen by physical eyes.)

If Ethel Romig Fuller will forgive my "tinkering" with her beautiful poem, I'll change it to read:

If radio's slim fingers can pluck a melody
From the night, and toss it over a continent,
    or sea;
If the petaled white notes of a violin
Are blown across a mountain or a city's din;
If songs, like crimson roses are culled from
    thin blue air,
Why should we wonder that the saints hear
    our prayers?

In Rodgers and Hammerstein's *The Sound of Music*, Hollywood star Julie Andrews sang, "Mi is a name I call myself." How fascinating that this pulsing blob of protoplasm called "Me" is invited to reach up and touch the face of God, link arms with His loved ones, and talk with them—all through the miracle of prayer.

I'm certain that Father James J. Daly, S.J., will not object to my changing his poem to read:*

> Our vigil is with the stars; our eyes are bright
> With radiance of them. Mystically slow
> Is their processional, while far below,
> Rome's quick and dead sleep—fellows
>   in the night.
> These very stars had marched in cryptic rite
> For Virgil in clear evening long ago,
> Gliding, like motes, athwart the overflow
> Of splendor from immortal tides of Light.
>
> What is this ant-life on a sphere of sand
> That it must drive, with ant-like cares, my soul
> Than all the stars together more sublime?
> So in the spacious night we plan our
>   spacious morrows—
> Centuries our scroll, upon a background
>   of Eternal Time
> While we speak with loved ones with us always.

The inspiring people of history need not remain mere names in a textbook. You can talk to them as you would your friends, for such, indeed, they are.

Link arms with King Tut, Dr. Wernher von Braun, and Bing Crosby, and stroll with them down the highway of time.

Perhaps experiences such as these strike you as "Strange Encounters of a Most Unusual Kind," but the fact is that each of us in our tiny portion of the globe can reach out and talk in prayer directly to such people as Louis Pasteur, and Pope John Paul I.

These excursions into prayer are not the only "Strange Encounters of a Most Unusual Kind," in our lives. Shortly after World War I, when I was a young boy attending the Immaculate Conception grade school in Butte, Montana, if someone had told us that one day we could sit in our living rooms and listen to a man speaking to them from the moon, we would have thought the idea impossible.

But on Sunday, July 20, 1969, thanks to the magic of TV, people on planet earth saw and heard two Americans speaking to us from the surface of the moon.

The universe is filled with magical things patiently waiting for us to discover them. "To be surprised, to wonder," says Jose Ortega y Gasset, "is to begin to understand."

And remember, "Calls to Saints" are "Zero-Plus" and "WATS." (You dial these calls yourself without charge to you.) The area code is H-E-A-V-E-N.

It may be a staggering thought for you to realize that we may be on a first-name basis with the truly great and inspiring people of history.

One of the joys of heaven will be the privilege to visit with these outstanding people in person and listen to them speak to us. But—and here is the overpowering truth—you don't have to wait until heaven to talk to your future companions. You may start now to enjoy their companionship in this life.

KING TUTANKHAMUN

Golden Memories

King Tutankhamun, you first flashed across my horizon like a blazing comet when I was nine years old, in the winter of 1922. It was on November 26, 1922, when British Egyptologist, Howard Carter, and his wealthy patron, Lord Carnarvon, discovered your tomb in the Valley of the Kings. Although you, Tutankhamun, were a pharoah who had ruled only nine years and died under mysterious circumstances at the age of 18 in 1350 B.C., you became extraordinarily appealing.

The treasures that were once in your 3,300-year-old tomb have been shown to packed museums around the world, and have inspired countless designers of art, jewelry and fashion over the decades. Hieroglyphs, geometrics and other Egyptian themes adorn sheets, games, puzzles, rugs, glasses, ice buckets, stationery, scarves, tote bags, trays, hairdos, plates, pots and posters.

Your enduring allure, King Tut, was proven by the "Treasures of Tutankhamun" which toured the U.S. After a three-year, seven-city tour, the treasures had been seen by an estimated seven million Americans.

When the treasures were on display in Chicago's Field Museum of Natural History, they drew a record crowd of 1,349,724 visitors. That figure could have been doubled if the museum had been able to handle the crowds. Seattle's Art Museum drew 1,293,203. When the show packed up, Seattle stores ran, "Goodbye, Tut" sales.

The incredible beauty and ageless craftsmanship accounted largely for the drawing power of your treasures, King Tut. The funeral mask alone is a majestic work. Your treasures are so fresh—according to Thomas Hoving, former director of the Metropolitan Museum of Art in New York, and the man who headed the team that organized the exhibition, "Treasures of Tutankhamun"—that "they kind of wipe out time."

Alice J. Hall, writing of your treasures in the *National Geographic* magazine, said, "Seeing them, we of the 20th century can reach across time and space to feel the pulse and spirit of an ancient people."

One of the most thrilling experiences of my life was when I was given the golden opportunity of visiting your tomb, King Tut. My trip went into high gear the moment I stepped into the railway depot in Cairo, Egypt. I thought for a moment I was viewing a real-life motion picture or a Hollywood extravaganza. Hundreds of white robed, turbaned Egyptians were trying to board a train that could only comfortably accommodate one third of the vast throng that surged towards the coaches.

In Egypt I found that men still wear robes called *galabias*. Some of the robes were white; others long since had given up any hope of being washed. Although the robes reached to the ankle and looked highly cumbersome, I found that men quickly cleared for action by taking the bottom hem in their teeth.

And action there was a plenty. Many men, in no hope of entering the train via the "jam-packed" doors, simply climbed in through the open windows.

When the interior of the train was packed as a sardine can, the rest of the crowd climbed to the top of the coaches and squatted on the roof. With their turbans and robes they looked like a flock of giant birds roosting in the sky.

The train I rode from Cairo south to Luxor ran parallel to the Nile and afforded me an opportunity to see the "miracle" wrought by this precious "stream of life."

According to Thomas J. Abercrombie, "In richness of history, no nation on earth can rival the long, continuous pageant that is Egypt, and no river reflects greater glory or greater toil than her Mother Nile. The ruined dreams of pharoahs and hovels of humble farmers alike lie buried along her banks. Here and there massive monuments still guard the greatness of darkly distant ages."

The Nile is the only conqueror of the Sahara. It is the sole source of life, and the chief artery of movement for the people of the lands it traverses.

Life of necessity clings to the banks of the Nile. Ninety-five percent of Egypt's forty million people live along the Nile. There are places where the irrigated fields seem to broaden out for leagues. Then, suddenly, the desert forces its way right down to the river bank, as if mad to drink.

The Nile is often below the level of the fields, so long-robed men in turbans spend their day "walking" up huge wooden wheels that slowly and laboriously lift precious water in clumsy buckets and dump it onto the thirsty soil.

As I looked out over the fields, King Tut, I felt as though I were back centuries in both time and space. Instead of a tractor, a water buffalo was pulling an ancient, wooden plow.

A solemn, swaying, deliberate camel, dignified even under its mountainous load of sugar cane, walked majestically after his long-gowned owner. A turbaned figure sat way aft on a sturdy little donkey, his legs too long for his mount.

Two women in flowing black—balancing great water jugs on their heads—walked to the river bank to fill their jars or *ballas* whose shapes have remained unchanged from Biblical days.

A kneeling figure, facing east, dropped to the attitude of prayer, head touching the earth. It was all a page right out of the past.

Luxor has been called "the true heart of ancient Egypt." Within a short walk of the railroad depot I saw the great colonnades that recall the monumental majesty that once was Luxor in the golden age of Egypt's power under Amenophis III in the 14th century B.C. A staff of 2,623 slaves once served in this 853-foot-long temple.

The temple wasn't the only ancient thing I found in Luxor. I needed a taxi, but instead I found myself riding in a battered old carriage pulled by two bony horses that looked like ghosts from the reign of Queen Hatshepsut at Deir el Bahri.

As the flea-bitten animals clip-clopped down the dusty street, we had to stop twice—once to let a flock of goats pass by, and another time to give way to a camel caravan.

I crossed the Nile in a battered, water-weary boat that looked as though it might gurgle out of sight at any moment and vanish in the muddy Nile.

The ancient pharoahs who picked the Valley of the Kings for their burial chambers chose a land that looks more like the landscape of the moon than planet earth.

Nothing grows in the rocky, barren wasteland. The sun-baked, sun-dried hills never know the pitter patter of rain in the valley.

Raindrops are so unusual in this high, dry land, that their presence becomes an historical event. If we go back into antiquity we find it recorded with wonder, "in this king's time, it rained."

I entered the various tombs of the kings through long corridors or tunnels that slope steeply into the rocky hillside.

The first thought that struck me as I walked down into the earth, was that of wonder. How were the workmen so many centuries before Christ able to cut through such mountains of solid rock, and make corridors straight and smooth? These ancient craftsmen had no power tools, no electric lights to work by. Yet the underground chambers they hewed out of the interior of the mountains are masterpieces. The spacious underground rooms with their lofty ceilings represent an engineering triumph of centuries long ago.

The tombs of the kings are monuments to immortality. They testify to the Egyptian's belief of life beyond the grave. The beautiful paintings on the walls of the tombs and along the corridors, show a people bounding with zest and joy, yet people who looked beyond this life to a greater life to come.

According to Rosemary Clark of Chicago, "The Egyptians were the most religious civilization the world has ever known. They believed very strongly in rebirth and resurrection."

Egyptian art depicts the eternal nature of things. The ancient artists interpret life as very beautiful. All is eternal, serene. Their way of life was an attempt to blend heaven with the best of earth, now, and throughout eternity.

Such an outlook—harmonizing man, nature, and the supernatural—produced a people who were basically happy and diligent. From the mightiest ruler to the humblest peasant, they wished for nothing more in the afterlife than a continuation of the joys they knew in this life...the joys of home and a loving family...of loafing in the shade of a tree at noon...of sitting down to supper after a hard day's work...of fondling the neck of a kitten or puppy...of watching children at play.

The pharoahs, alas, made one mistake. They put into their tombs vast treasures of gold, gems, and art. This, ironically, became their own undoing. Had the pharoahs been buried without any treasures, they might have rested in their tombs undisturbed for ages.

Century after century, tomb robbers were lured by the prospect of buried treasure. The guide showed me where robbers of long centuries past had burrowed with primitive tools and flickering lamps through vaults and yards of solid rock, past labyrinths of blind alleys and false passages, deep pits and bars of iron, until, at last, they reached a majestic monarch wrapped in shrouds, and surrounded by gleaming gold.

Only one pharoah out of many scores seems to have escaped spoliation by robbers, and this pharoah is you, King Tut. Your tomb is the only one in the Luxor area that archaeologists found largely intact. The nearly 5,000 works of art taken from your tomb gives the world some idea of the incredible riches stolen from tombs of older, greater kings.

After visiting the burial chambers of the kings, deep inside the hillside, I walked up the long tunnel and out into the blinding sunlight. I was approximately 450 miles south of Cairo and was at the base of the great cliff known as Deir el Bahri that leaps up in a dynamic crescendo to the sky.

Now came my "Moment of Truth"—the climax of my entire trip to Egypt, my visit to your tomb, King Tut. As I walked down the gravel path leading to the stone steps that descend into your tomb, the blood vessels in my temples were ticking like metronomes. Trumpets and cymbals seemed to ring in my head with all the overtones of an echo chamber.

As I bent down to enter into your burial chambers, King Tut, I experienced something of the thrill that overcame Carter and Carnarvon when they beheld the vases in alabaster, chariots overlaid in gold, gilded couches, and a large sculpture in black wood of the jackal god Anubis lying upon an elevated pedestal. The head was held high, watchful; the ears were erect, listening.

Although most of the treasures from your tomb, King Tut, have been taken to the Museum in Cairo, it was still exciting to visit your tomb. I was amazed at how bright and clear the paintings on the walls are after all these thousands of years. The jewel-like irides-cent colors applied to the walls of the tomb over twelve centuries before Christ, still speak their message crisp and clear, filling the air, as it were, with clear, bell-like sounds almost like the shimmer of crystal.

Through the medium of picture language, I felt as though I heard the dreams and shared the joy of your people of long ago. I felt as though I were "shaking hands" with the unknown, talented artists of centu-ries past.

The cosmic stretch of over 30 centuries seemed to fade into nothingness when I looked at the wall paint-ings and realized that the thoughts they evoked in my mind were first faint stirrings in the brain of a gifted artist many hundreds of years ago. No wonder a poet said:*

A thing of beauty is a joy forever;
Its loveliness increases; it will never
Pass into nothingness; but still will keep
A bower quiet for us, and sleep
Full of sweet dreams, and health,
    and quiet breathing.

—John Keats

As I walked through the chamber that once held your innermost coffin with its golden effigy of you as a boy-king, I began thinking of the lesson you were silently relaying to me, King Tut.

Once upon a time you enjoyed the four S's of Egypt—cloudless skies, clean sands, clear seas, and sharp sun, 365 days a year. But then, no doubt, there were days when wires of pain jerked your nerves, and your head was split by an ax of pain. Perhaps your stomach felt as though you were being branded with a red hot iron. Each hour seemed an eternity, and you asked, "Will this pain ever end?"

Now, King Tut, as you look back over the centuries, you realize full well that the pain did end. The lesson you give us is simple: "The sufferings of this time are not to be compared to the glory that is to come."

The example of your life, King Tut, proves that "Pain is passing. Joy is lasting."

For us in the 20th century there are times when tension, sorrow, fear, and anxiety build up like high pressure steam in a boiler until we seem about to "blow our tops."

When pain cuts like a razor blade into our flesh, and our heads feel like a keg of TNT about to explode, we can do well, King Tut, to think of you, and remember that for us, also, will come a day when weeping, and suffering will be things of the past. Then, from our own vantage point beyond the grave, we will look back and realize that pain is limited and ends.

It is important to note that this lesson you give us, King Tut, does not do away with pain, or lessen it. Religion does not do away with the hard, cold, cruel facts of suffering that jut into our lives like granite cliffs, or that rise up like giant rocks to impede our forward motion, and make us stumble, or block our path entirely.

The late Pope John XXIII was a man of joy and of hope. He was also a man of truth, and with utmost honesty he admitted that even in the best of lives we frequently find ourselves in a tunnel of darkness, suffering, and agony that seems to lead nowhere but to another tunnel of its own. Each hour of suffering seems to be a lifetime. We even crave unconsciousness. With Longfellow we ask the night to lay its fingers on the lips of care, until they care no more.

The North American Martyrs said they would rather experience at once the sharp impact of the Indian tomahawk on their skulls than endure the deadly stench, smoke, and dirt of the wigwams in the dead of winter.

William Shakespeare's *Portia* complained that her little body was weary of this great world. A modern, 20th century woman wrote that on her wedding day she was bubbling with joy. "From now on," she said, "I will never be lonely. I have a husband who loves me very much. Each morning my Prince Charming will place a kiss on my lips and I will be happy throughout the day."

Alas, there came a terrible shock. Despite her Prince Charming, there were still times when she experienced the chilling sensation of loneliness. Only now, the loneliness was worse than before. Her expectations had been dashed to pieces. She had discovered that no shining knight on a white horse can deliver a happy-ever-after gift neatly tied with pink ribbon.

At times, no doubt, we all experience what Antoinette Bosco calls, "an occasional overwhelming dismalness about life."

At such times our prayer becomes that of Cardinal Newman, considered by many to be the first man of letters of his time.

Lead, kindly Light, amid the encircling gloom,*
    Lead Thou me on!
The night is dark, and I am far from home—
    Lead Thou me on!
Keep Thou my feet; I do not ask to see

The distant scene,—one step enough for me.
I was not ever thus, nor prayed that Thou
   Shouldst lead me on;
I loved the garish day, and, spite of fears,
Pride ruled my will: remember not past years!
So long Thy power has blest me, sure it still
   Will lead me on
O'er moor and fen, o'er crag and torrent, till
   The night is gone;
And with the morn those angel faces smile
Which I have loved long since, and lost awhile!

To make the leap from the poetical to the practical, I call for help upon Charles Hunter, S.J. Father Hunter is a Jesuit priest working in Belize City, Belize, Central America. In a Christmas letter to me, Father Hunter said, "Our headmaster asked me to give the homily at our graduation Mass at St. John's this year. He surprised me by pointing out that this year marked the 50th anniversary of my own graduation from old St. John's of Loyola Park in 1928!

"The mention of the fact evoked from the assembly a reaction of reverent applause to which I responded with what hoary-headed good advice I could summon from my half-century of experience. Boiled down, it amounted to this: don't dote too much on the past; don't worry too much about the future; learn the quiet art of paying attention to what you're doing while putting your trust in God and your heart in the job before you. How prosaic can you be! But practical, I hope."

By dying at an early age, King Tut, you escaped the one thing that many people fear most. According to the National Institute on Aging, many people fear old age more than death itself. These people wish for shorter lives than they think await them. They would rather die earlier than later. They want to avoid what William Shakespeare called the last stage of life, or "second childishness," in which we end up "*sans* teeth, *sans* eyes, *sans* taste, *sans* everything." (*Sans* is a French word for "without.")

Today in rest homes across the world are people who are confined to a bed of pain. Their world is bounded by the walls of their room, and the sides of their beds. Time and again I've heard these poor people complain, "Why can't I die?" "How much longer do I have to live?"

You, King Tut, teach us that no matter how long our pain-filled nights, a new dawn will come. This beautiful truth is captured for us by Michael Kent in his beautiful and inspiring book, *The Mass of Brother Michael*.

"Tomorrow we lay aside these garments we have worn on earth, and in their place, what glory we shall receive! Tomorrow heaven is ours, and beauty, and an end of pain, forever. I cannot think what it will be like to live without pain, but tomorrow it will be as if it had never been. And in proportion as we have suffered on earth, for Love, so much greater will our joy be in heaven. We have great happiness here, it is true; but on earth it is broken and interrupted. Tomorrow we will receive that joy in all its fullness, and it will never end. Tomorrow we do not die, Louise, we live."

A great seventeenth century Englishman, Thomas Traherne, wrote, "Your enjoyment of the world is never right until every morning you wake up in heaven."

"There is a great degree of happiness, and that fairly continuous," remarks Clare Boothe Luce, "in being mindful of Him (God). If you keep Him in mind, yours will be often the happy mood of the poet:

'To see the world in a grain of sand,
And heaven in a wild flower;
Hold infinity in the palm of your hand,
And eternity in an hour.'"

Written on the great golden shrine surrounding your sarcophagus, King Tut, are words which some scientists think may be your very own, "I have seen yesterday; I know tomorrow."

We too, expect one day to repeat that phrase. In the meantime, we keep in mind the words of Father Albert J. Nimeth, O.F.M., "Keep your faith in God above. We will meet again in everlasting love."

ARISTOTLE

The Magnetism of Beauty

It was in your homeland, Aristotle, that I experienced the strange sensation of being at home away from home. When I climbed to the top of the island of rock known as the Acropolis, that rises like a giant's thumb in the center of Athens, even though I was thousands of miles from the good, old U.S.A., I felt perfectly at home.

To my right on the highest point of the plateau or table of rock rose the ancient Greek temple known as the Parthenon. This doric temple to Athena was built in the 5th century B.C. by the great Phidias. The Parthenon has been described as "man's victory over matter." According to Felix Marti-Ibanez, the Parthenon is "a marble harp suspended from the radiant blue, an eternal symbol of the Greek miracle."

To my left was a smaller building known as the Erechtheion. On the south of this building is a small porch supported by Caryatids, marble figures of maidens with serene eyes and crescent smiles. The Caryatids stand like figures in a dream, six beautiful girls with one knee advancing under the pleats of their dresses, as though halting for a moment in a procession. On their lips is a smile. On their heads they balance baskets, filled with wheat offerings to the goddess, Athena. They support the wall above them as lightly as a garland.

The buildings on the Athenian Acropolis are considered to be the supreme architectural achievement of the supreme city in the Greek world at the height of its wealth and power.

Around me on all sides walked dozens of tourists. Never have I seen so many people make so little noise. Some of the people sat on the marble steps and read their guide books to identify the lovely scenes before them. Others simply walked in silence, or stood lost in contemplation of the overpowering beauty.

Everyone seemed caught up in a tidal wave of beauty, and they hesitated to speak lest they shatter and dispel the radiance in which they were immersed.

The reason I felt so perfectly at home on the Acropolis is that I had been looking at pictures of this lovely spot almost every year since I started school.

When I was a young boy I looked at pictures of the buildings on the Acropolis in my geography books and history books. When I went to the Christian Brothers High School in Butte, and later, to Creighton Prep in Omaha, Nebraska, I saw still more pictures in my ancient history books, and in my religion books. (With the coming of Christianity, the Parthenon was turned into a Catholic Church dedicated to our Blessed Mother. It served this purpose for many years.)

When I began college in Florissant, Missouri, I was launched into my study of the Greek language, Greek history, and Greek archealogy. I became as familiar with the geography of the Acropolis as I did the backyard of my former home. No wonder I felt at home.

Finally, when I began the study of philosophy at St. Louis University, St. Louis, Missouri, I was introduced, Aristotle, to your tremendous contributions to the human race. You and your fellow Greeks opened up to me a world of order, beauty and truth.

Your teacher, Plato, insisted that all knowledge came from within. You, Aristotle, contended that everything emanates from the outside and is absorbed through the senses. Time and again I have recalled your famous statement, "Nothing is in the intellect unless it has first been in the senses." Only through our senses—seeing, hearing, smelling, touching and tasting—do we gain knowledge of ourselves and the world around us.

Our brains are locked up in silent darkness inside the bony walls of our skulls, and have to depend on the five senses to bring information about the great wide world that surrounds us.

Even knowledge of God comes to us through our senses. The very first time mother whispered the word "God," His name came to us by means of sound waves, vibrating molecules of air that moved the eardrum. And when we read the word "God" on this page, we are actually looking at three letters from the alphabet. A tiny word made from molecules of paper and ink that speaks to us of Him who lights the stars in the heavens, and who walks upon the wings of the wind.

I was lucky, Aristotle, in having outstanding teachers who were convinced that Greek literature, art and philosophy—with their accent on beauty and truth—are our most precious heirloom.

Your fellowmen, along with you, taught us that man needs to see beauty, and the more beauty we see, the more beautiful we become. The beauty of the world and the beauty of man reflect the beauty of God. The more we see of this beauty, the closer we will be to seeing the beauty of God.

One of my most outstanding teachers, the late Father J. Castiello, S.J., emphasized again and again that nothing is so refining as beauty. With beauty, life is pleasant and joyful. Without it, life becomes hard and bleak.

It is, therefore, of the utmost importance that beauty should play a large part in the education of children and that educational institutions should use this most powerful medium to make truth and goodness lovable.

Is not the strange power which such great universities as Oxford or Cambridge, Heidelberg, Bonn or Princeton exert on their students due, in part at least, to the charm and refinement of their buildings, their life, and their culture?

Just as an artist loves a certain ideal of beauty, so too in the domain of morality, people have a certain ideal of moral goodness, which they derive from nature, from experience of other people's virtues and heroism, and from their own innate desire of righteousness.

No one takes pains to beautify that for which he or she has no regard or respect. It is a well known fact that artists have a special appreciation for the raw stuffs of their trades. They see their possibilities.

Something similar happens to us. We see our possibilities. A real sense of one's own moral value is a great stimulant to moral goodness. On the other hand, there is nothing more stunting than an inferiority complex, that latent persuasion that one is useless in life. Hence the wisdom in stressing one's own importance and cultivating self-respect.

We must love ourselves, and we can love ourselves only if we appreciate our true worth. This is not a case of fomenting pride or priggishness. There is nothing more healthy than a certain amount of conscious efficiency.

The real basis of our self-respect is that we are children of God. Even if we are powerless in human affairs, we still have before us the infinite possibilities of the moral order. A sick person or a stupid person may be useless for man, but such people are never useless for God.

To be great citizens in the kingdom of God, we need only do our small daily tasks here and now, day by day.

A government bond is valuable not because it is printed on expensive paper, but because it gives a title to a certain amount of money. Our daily actions likewise are of value, not because they are world conquering events in themselves, but because they are the bonds of good deeds which give us a title to tremendous treasures in the kingdom of heaven.

When we offer up our daily prayer, works and sufferings to God, then the events of the day become chains of gold binding our hands to the hands of God. The credit we build up by doing our daily tasks the way God wants them performed gives us great purchasing power in the kingdom of heaven. Each day we deposit the credit of our good works in the First National Bank of Heaven.

Each day we can store up for ourselves treasures in heaven, where rust does not consume, nor thieves steal. Each day can be an expression of love for God.

It is interesting to note that people can love intensely that which they hardly understand, if it is presented to them in a beautiful form. Art makes things easy to contemplate and irresistibly lovable. The conclusion we may draw from this fact is as obvious as it is important. Since young people cannot understand many things from sheer lack of maturity, parents and teachers should start off by helping them to love that which they are to understand later: virtue and science, man and nature, and, above all, God.

The moment we start to beautify something, in that very instant we have ceased to be selfish. The "humane" person gives to everything he does a finish, a touch of perfection, which are a joy to himself, and to all those who know him. Such people care for their own person, their own mind, for what they write and say, for their home and garden, for their friends and for the land they live in. They love and are unselfish.

It is most important that parents train their children to love beauty and to give beauty not only in the material sphere, but also in the moral and social. Heroism is simply moral beauty. Thus the cult of the beautiful, when carried out in a healthy virile way, is the most social of all training. It is a training for unselfishness.

One's work is the reflection of one's own self. The person who sees the seal of his own personality in his work, acquires a sense of power. Pathologists know this so well that they use work as an instrument of remedial treatment, and, as has been shown again and again, with great success. Give a person a certain sense of power, and he or she is a new individual.

Parents and teachers who are inspired, and who can make that which they teach lovable, will exert a life-long influence on their young charges.

As you found out, Aristotle, from your teacher, Plato, all creative activity is born of love. The fundamental phenomenon of creative genius is the thirst, the yearning for beauty born of a dim intuition of its loveliness.

Artists wield the most powerful of all educational instruments, namely, that loveliness which conquers the hearts of all because it fixes indelibly what it touches and perpetuates it for always.

No wonder it has been said that "We are shaped and fashioned by what we love."

According to Frithjof Schuon, "Beauty is in our very being; we live on the substance of it. It is the calm and simple, yet generous and unlimited perfection of the pond in which is reflected the serenity of the sky; it is the beauty of the water lily, of the lotus which opens to the light."

John Muir told us, "Everybody needs beauty as well as bread, places to play in and pray in, where nature may heal and cheer and give strength to body and soul alike."

And John Ruskin would have us keep in mind that "Nature is painting for us, day after day, pictures of infinite beauty if only we have the eyes to see them."

Helen Keller was once asked what she thought was the worst calamity to befall a person. She answered, "To have eyes and fail to see."

The world is too big to be taken in at one glance. The second look may sharpen details and bring to attention details we would have missed. The wonderful gift or power of seeing our everyday world in a rewarding and unique way is the result of what the famous photographer, Ernst Haas, calls "dreaming with your eyes open."

Children often have this ability to see beauty that escapes adults, for they still "dream with their eyes open." After a rain a little girl said to her mother, "Oh look, Mommy, there's a rainbow in the gutter!"

"That's not a rainbow, silly," her mother corrected her. "That's a dirty oil slick."

Truly, if adults had the seeing eyes of a small child, they would have a different outlook on life.

George Washington Carver was vividly alive to God's beauty all around him. He said, "I love to think of nature as an unlimited broadcasting station, through which God speaks to us every hour, if we only will tune in."

Wheeler McMillen tells us, "I am 86, the calendar says. And isn't this a wonderful world to be alive in? I marvel and marvel.

"I pluck a flower and marvel at stem and stamens, pistil and petal, all the delightful and complicated beauty within and without.

"There's a bug! Who could make one? What an endless diversity ingenious insects present to us!

"To each precious day the grace of birds lends enchantment with all their color and vivacity.

"I marvel at the farms out in the open country, at their beauty and bounty, at their ceaseless output of essential foods."**

Two years before I visited your lovely country, Aristotle, I was given a trip to the Land of the Rising Sun. The one thing that impressed me most about Japan is that the people know and appreciate the value of beauty.

Many of the people are poor in this world's goods, but never have I seen people make so much with so little, and with such a delicate taste for beauty and the refining things of life.

In the villages and on the farms I saw people working long, hard hours to secure the meager necessities of life. But the people are alive and vibrant to the refining influence of beauty. A Japanese girl is taught from childhood the satisfaction of doing something for its own sake. She is taught the art of flower arrangement—both to create a composition of beauty, and to achieve, while doing it, contentment and serenity of mind.

Parents take obvious delight in their children. And when children go visiting, they dress neatly—crisp and delightful to behold as a gladiolus. Though their clothes are of common, ordinary material, they are clean and fresh as dawn. The youngsters radiate the pride their parents take in them.

When I purchased some postcards, the clerk wrapped them in such beautiful and exquisite paper, and tied them with such artistic ribbons, I wanted to keep the creation intact as a souvenir of beauty.

The Fujita bus I took from Tokyo to Hakone was beyond all compare. Not only was it clean and bright as a pearl, but it was the first bus I had ever seen that had fresh flowers carefully arranged in holders on the wall!

"The contemplation of the beautiful," remarked John Ruskin, "is a necessary part of life. What we like determines what we are." The people I met in Japan may never have read Ruskin, but they prove his wise observations by their daily lives.

Before I left your city, Aristotle, I walked from the Acropolis to the place where St. Paul is reported to have stood when he talked to the people of Athens. A massive bronze marker set into a huge rock commemorates the place where St. Paul stood when he said, "Men of Athens, as I walked around looking at your shrines, I even discovered an altar inscribed, 'To a God Unknown.' Now, what you are thus worshiping in ignorance I intend to make known to you. For the God who made the world and all that is in it, the Lord of heaven and earth, does not dwell in sanctuaries made by human hands.... It is He who gives to all life and breath and everything else.... 'In Him we live and move and have our being'" (Acts 17:22-25, 28).

CICERO

The Magic of Words

The oldest letter I ever read, Cicero, was one written by you many centuries ago.

Bright and early on my first morning in Rome I had the golden opportunity of visiting the most important library in the world. The Vatican Library is so rated, not particularly for the number of its books, but for the value of its ancient manuscripts which embrace every phase and aspect of civilization.

The centuries seemed to roll away when I looked into glass cases and saw manuscripts and letters that date back many long centuries. The reason that your letter fascinated me most of all, Cicero, is that I looked upon it as a personal message coming from an old friend. After all, I had spent many long hours in high school and college translating your glorious words from Latin into English.

As I looked at the letter you wrote approximately half a century before the birth of Christ, I was struck with the wonder of words. How could anything so flat, and black and white fill my head with excitement, and make my pulse beat faster?

I recalled what Lewis Carroll wrote at the beginning of *Alice in Wonderland*, "The magic words shall hold thee fast." Words are vehicles that can transport us from the drab sands to the dazzling stars.

The individual letters of the alphabet are made up of molecules of ink placed on molecules of paper. Of themselves they are merely marks. A "P" or "C" or "A" in itself fails to stir the imagination. But when the letters of the alphabet arrange themselves in the proper sequence, behold the magic. The above-mentioned letters hold hands to form the word "CAP."

And then, more miracles! Isolated words in a dictionary or speller stand alone. On a printed page, the words sweep into action. "The bearded man pulled his fur cap down over his ears, and strode out into the storm blowing down from the North."

Each time I open a new book I experience a deep tremor of awe, of joy and delightful anticipation. I smooth out the first page in a gesture of beginning.

Words are not simply things in themselves but keys to ideas. Every word and every sentence is a tool for unlocking minds. And once the mind is unlocked, it becomes the doorway to ever-widening vistas of knowledge.

Jonathan Swift once referred to the "artillery of words." This phrase has vital meaning. To win a battle in which words are artillery and ideas have the impact of missiles, we need minds of broad caliber and depths of intellect.

It is true that words are only black marks on paper or sounds in the air, but think of the power they have. Words can make people laugh or cry, love or hate, fight or run away; they can heal or hurt.

It is interesting to note, Cicero, that the regulation or rule for good public speaking is the same today as it was in your time. The method today, as always, is imagery. The only way people can see what the speaker is talking about is when he gives them in fact, something to see, namely, language that is highly visual.

According to Felix Marti-Ibanez, words are swift little birds that fly from a mouth or from paper into the ear or eye of the listener or reader, and after singing their song of beauty, they continue their flight to other ears or eyes. If atoms are centers of energy, words are the retreat where the poet's ideas nest.

A writer uses words to hammer on the doors of our minds to pound home his idea. A poet submerges himself in the abyss of his being, he embraces his "I" with cosmic hunger, he peers into the swirling waters of his soul to discover the whole reflected universe.

The year 1948 marked my first year of teaching at Campion High School, Prairie du Chien, Wisconsin. It also marked the start of the Wisconsin Rural Writers' Association. Their "Creed" was simple and beautiful: "Man's deepest experience of life is essentially solitary; at the same time he desires to communicate to others his moments of intense feeling, his present experience, the rich memories of the past.

"Let us believe in each other, remembering each has tasted the bitter with the sweet, sorrow with gladness, toil with rest. Let us believe in ourselves and our talents. Let us believe in the worth of the individual and seek to understand him...whether he be great or small, young or old, rash or deliberate, brilliant or plodding...for from sympathy and understanding will our writings grow.

"Let us believe that the mark of the cultured man is the ability to express himself competently in language. This ability can be gained best through study and application."

I once had two interesting experiences, both based on the wonder of words. Father William Barnaby Faherty, S.J., invited me to come to the Metropolitan College of Saint Louis University to give the luncheon talk to the Writer's Workshop. The title of my talk was "Adventures in Writing."

Immediately following this talk, a tall, distinguished looking gentleman came up and introduced himself to me. He was Mr. Nade O. Peters from the McDonnell Douglas Corporation. In his quiet, winning manner, Mr. Peters explained to me that he was the Program Chairman for the 24th International Technical Communication Conference, which would meet in the Pick Congress Hotel in Chicago in May, and he was offering me the honor of giving the keynote address.

So it came to pass, that in the huge, spacious ballroom of the Pick Congress Hotel, I gave the keynote address to attendees from all areas of the United States and many countries outside the U.S. It was one of the most thrilling moments in my life.

The title of my talk was, "The Wonder of Words— an Adventure in Technical Communication." What follows constitutes about one half that talk.

"If you have ideas running around inside your head, how do you capture them, wrap them up, and ship them off into the mind of your neighbor? In short, how do we communicate?

"A poet once wrote, 'Let me count the ways I love thee.' Today we can also say, 'Let me count the ways we communicate.'

"Before *Roots* flashed across millions of television screens, it first glimmered as an idea in the mind of Alex Haley. He ensnared his ideas in a magic web of words in his magnificent book of 688 absorbing pages.

"Before the Saturn rocket leaped up from the Kennedy Space Center to hurl our astronauts to the moon, the rocket existed as an idea in the mind of Doctor Wernher von Braun. He captured his ideas in the delicate outlines of blueprints, drawings, and sketches, and then brought them into existence.

"An artist, such as Raphael, used paint and brush to capture his ideas on a canvas that explodes with life and vibrancy.

"Matthew Brady found the new thing called a 'camera' to record the Civil War in stark but shadowy reality so that the future could never forget what it was really like in those dark days.

"Signs and symbols express our ideas—NASA, MGM, GE, STC, the Liberty Bell, and those utterly fascinating symbols on a dollar bill.

"Even a piece of cloth can stand for an idea. The American flag is merely a cloth of red, white, and blue, but it speaks to us of the ideals of liberty and freedom that have made us the United States.

"Most of our communication is done through our words. 'At the sound of your voice,' sang Mario Lanza, 'heaven opens its portals to me.' How truly marvelous that emotions quivering with desire, ideas dynamic as a Saturn rocket, thought subtle as cosmic rays...can be caught and put into words—and air waves, matter in motion, molecules on the go. Millions of tiny molecules of air, bits of matter set into motion by your vocal cords, tongue, and lips vibrate against an eardrum—and there is magic in your day.

"The miracle that is speech intrigues Professor Lans-Lukas Teuber of M.I.T's Department of Psychology. He says, 'What fascinates me is the way you and I are able to sit opposite each other and make sounds that each receives, decodes, processes, and then uses as a basis for making more sounds. Now that is a *real* mystery!'

"According to my good friend, Father Walter Ong, S.J., 'What words do is precisely annihilate the inbetweenness which separates you from me. When I speak to you, I am inviting you to enter into my consciousness, and I am entering yours. Words are invitations to sharing.'

"The magic of words! Listen to Marshall Patain at Verdun—'Ils ne passeront pas.' (They shall not pass). Four words to revive a faltering nation; to stiffen a stumbling army.

"Hear General MacArthur in the darkest days of our World War II loss of the Philippines—'I shall return.' Three words. Three words to signify the united intent of 150 million Americans. And sharpen your ear to catch General MacAuliffe's single word in the bitter wind and snows of Bastogne in December of 1944—"Nuts!" Not too technical perhaps, but the general left the German courier no doubt of the communication aspect of his reply to the surrender demand.

"Nothing else makes communication as easy as do words. Writing and print give words a marvelous potential. From ancient writings on soft clay to the invention of moveable metal type, and down to the 20th century, the fascination of the written word has captivated man. Libraries rely on the printed word. No values can be cherished long without the ministry of words. Historian Jacques Barzun reminds us that 'Truth cannot be told apart from the right words.'

"A writer is one of the greatest artists, and he needs only his dreams, a pencil stub, and a few sheets of paper to create a 'masterpiece.' The writer recreates his world, the world around him, and the world he carries within himself.

"One of the joys of life is the discovery of the exactly 'right' word—the word that is true and able to be shared. It brings an opening of mind and spirit in which we understand not only what we have in our minds, but what we have in each other's company. Words share the very life and spirit of the person who voices them. They are man's companion as he becomes a discoverer of reality.

"Communication depends primarily upon words. If you wish your readers to gambol barefoot in the rich meadows of metaphor; if you want them to sift through their fingers the rare coins of your syntax, then you must be a lover of words. Words are the gold coins, the precious medium of exchange in the world of communication. In *Time* Magazine for November 22, 1976, we read, 'In Franklin Roosevelt's time, words skillfully forged and used reached out across the nation through those cathedral radios and touched so many people that the anguish of the Great Depression gave way to new hope.' It is not inconceivable that when we look back to the Kennedy years, their greatest legacy will be the short phrase, 'the pursuit of excellence.' John Kennedy relished it, practiced it, made poetry out of it in speeches, and that inspiration still lives with us.

"According to a radio program on communication sponsored by Wisconsin University, 'The first thing in communication is awareness.' If we are to communicate, we must have something to say. We must have ideas worth sharing. To get these ideas, we must keep the windows of our minds open to the great world throbbing all around us; don't be so narrow-minded that you can look through a keyhole with both eyes. Rather, let your vision expand until its wonder is as wide as the universe itself. Great men have always stressed the value of wonder."

I wish, Cicero, that you had been with me on the evening I had the privilege of listening to one of America's outstanding platform personalities, Mr. George Walter. George is the greatest living artist I've ever heard who uses words to weave a web of magic and beauty. The arrows of his thoughts are winged and tipped with flame. His words lance the darkness of the night like Roman candles. They leap up in the midnight sky like skyrockets cascading golden sparks of beauty and truth.

At times George uses words like cannon balls to pound home his ideas. Then, again his words whisper, like a harp gently caressed.

No one merely sits back and listens passively to George. His exciting delivery jabs your attention like a harpoon. By the end of the lecture, every erg of energy has been drained. You are limp with astonishment and delight.

Reading is a key to knowledge. Mental stagnation will never set in as long as we keep the lamp of learning brightly burning in the house of the intellect. The benefits of reading include the development of ideals, sensitivity to ethical values, the acquisition of skills and insights, the experience of adventure, and a feel for beauty. Reading strikes the spark of enthusiasm and ignites the excitement of discovery. Andre Gide, the French novelist and Nobel prize winner for literature, was right: "The wise man is he who constantly wonders afresh."

Studies conducted at the University of Illinois indicate that the earlier you learn to read, the greater your capacity for achievement is likely to be.

Studies of youngsters, both British and American, have shown that those who read most in their out-of-school hours are most likely to be at the top of their classes. Those who spend more time watching TV tend to get lower grades.

The quality of thinking of a nation's people is closely related to the amount and kind of reading they do. Words are the tools of thought; vocabularies are built and language facility is gained largely by reading.

No wonder that William Arthur Ward, noted lecturer and speaker, said, "We have not completely fulfilled our responsibility as parents until we bequeath to our children a love of books, a thirst for knowledge, a hunger for righteousness, an awareness of beauty, a memory of kindness, an understanding of loyalty, a vision of greatness, and a good name."

You, Cicero, in your *Pro Archia*, gave us a beautiful commentary on books: "Books nourish our youthful minds and delight us in old age. They embellish prosperity, afford refuge in adversity, and give solace in loneliness. They delight us when we are at home, and never impede our journeys. They spend the night with us, go abroad with us, and accompany us into the country."

Congratulations to you, Cicero, on this neat summary on the value of books. Even though books don't talk, they have a lot to say. They give us the wisdom of great authors. They let us hear the beautiful sounds of our poets. They stimulate the mind and help us create images of any time, anywhere.

Books make it possible to live with the greatest men and women of every age. We can walk through the streets of ancient Athens listening to the voice of Aristotle. We can hear the lapping of the waters of the sea of Tiberius and sit at the feet of Christ. Lincoln is no farther away from us than our eyes and mind. At the windows of our soul are George Washington, Shakespeare, and Willa Cather waiting for a nod to show themselves to us.

Books are great people at their best. To live among them is to take on something of their greatness, to live in familiarity with the significant ideas which can make the world a decent place to live.

By rubbing elbows with the great personalities and the thoughts of literature, history, and science, we develop our imagination and thinking powers. We become much less at the mercy of life and circumstances. We have more intellectual capital to live on.

Any person can enjoy in the quiet of his or her home the companionship of the great souls of history. Even if we live in a modest home, we can have living with us prophets and philosophers, poets and preachers, kings and queens, heroes and martyrs.

No wonder that Waldemar Argow wrote, "This morning I walked with the gods! Not in Valhalla, but in the confines of my own room. Through the miracle of the printed word, I listened to the sage admonitions of Socrates, thrilled to the lyric beauty of Wordsworth and Coleridge, and sat in reverence at the feet of the great Hebrew prophets. All the wealth and the wisdom of five thousand years of intellectual achievement were mine through the pages of my open books."***

Good books live for all time and fire the hearts of men to high ideals and heroic duty. Our outlook on life is greatly influenced by what we read. For this reason we should read the best.

Winston Churchill was to the point when he said, "You feed a cow—why shouldn't you feed your mind? You cannot expect the poor animal to work unless it is refreshed by nourishment. And my advice is to make sure that you read the great books of the English language. Literature is one of our greatest sources of inspiration and of strength."

Thanks to books, we can spend an evening with George Washington and his fellow Presidents. We can listen to the voices of Valley Forge and of Yorktown; voices that ring like great bronze bells. We can touch down with our astronauts on our country's first lunar landing; blaze the trail to the West with Lewis and Clark. We can perfect a symphony with Beethoven; raise our country's flag with the heroes of Iwo Jima; feel the force of Michelangelo's genius.

The world's greatest writers have created stories that are immortal masterpieces, or works of such imaginative power that they have the force of actual experience. They have created works of such wit and wisdom that they illuminate the nature and the meaning of life; works of such rich variety, that they penetrate every aspect of human existence and have become part of the literary heritage of all mankind.

Thomas Carlyle reminds us that "All that mankind has said, done, thought, gained, or been, is lying as in magic preservation in the pages of books. They are the chosen possession of men."

And Ralph Waldo Emerson reminds us: "In the highest civilization the book is still the highest delight. He who has once known its satisfactions is provided with a resource against calamity."

Oliver Goldsmith said, "The first time I read an excellent book, it is to me just as if I had gained a new friend."

"A house without books," said Horace Mann, "is like a room without windows. No man has a right to bring up his children without surrounding them with books."

The University of California came up with some interesting studies which show that women who get the greatest enjoyment out of reading tend to be the easiest to get along with, and to be happier than women who don't care for reading. Psychological tests showed that they made the best companions, and are much more likely to be quiet-spoken, thoughtful, feminine, and agreeable.

On November 5, 1855, Abe Lincoln wrote a letter to Isham Reavis in which he said, "If you are resolutely determined to make a lawyer of yourself, the thing is more than half done already. Get the books and read and study them till you understand them. It is of no consequence to be in a large town while you are reading. I read at New Salem, which never had 300 people living in it. The books and your capacity for understanding them are just the same in all places."

Mark Twain was not a college man, but he was a highly educated man, largely because he was from boyhood an omniverous reader. He is said by some to be the most original of all American humorous writers because he had a well-fed mind and kept it well-fed to the end.

Books are passports to rich and varied experiences, to beauty and inspiration and lasting enjoyment.

I began this chapter, Cicero, speaking to you about your letter in the Vatican Library. One of the popes responsible for making Rome the center of letters is Leo X, who wrote, "I have been thoroughly convinced that next to the knowledge and worship of the Creator nothing is better or more useful for mankind than such studies, which are not only an advancement and a standard of human life, but also of service in every circumstance. In misfortune, books console us; in prosperity they confer joy and honor, and without them man would be robbed of all social class and culture."

"Hold fast to that which is good," said St. Paul, and no person today should be deprived of the memorable classics of literature.

"I cannot live without books," said Thomas Jefferson.

To me, Cicero, the most inspiring of your many writings are those concerned with death and our life to come. I especially like the following from your pen: "To me, nothing seems long to which there is an end. For when that end has arrived, then the time which has passed is gone at once; only so much remains as you have secured by virtue and good deeds; the hours depart, and the days and the months and the years, nor does the time that is past ever return.

"The nearer I approach to death, I seem to sight land as it were, and to be at last on the port of entering the harbor after a long voyage.

"I consider that your fathers, men of the highest renown and my dearest friends, are still living, and living moreover that life which alone deserves to be called life.

"In Xenophon, Cyrus the Elder on his deathbed speaks as follows: 'Do not think, my dearest sons, that I, when I shall have departed from you, shall be nowhere or nobody. When I was with you, you did not see my soul, but you knew from my actions that it was in my body. Believe, therefore, that it will still exist, though you do not see me.'

"I, for my part, am carried away by the desire of seeing your fathers, whom I have honored and loved; not indeed is it only those whom I myself have known, that I long to meet, but those too about whom I have heard and read, and have myself written.

"I depart life as from an inn, not as from a home, for it is as an hostelry for sojourning in, not as a place for dwelling in, that nature has assigned life to us. O glorious day, when I shall set out for that divine assemblage and company of souls and when I shall depart from this turmoil and confusion.

"For I shall set out not only to those men of whom I have before spoken, but also to my own son, than whom no better man or one more full of filial love was ever born.

"And this misfortune of mine, I appeared to bear up bravely against, not because I was bearing it with a tranquil mind, but I was in fact comforting myself by reflecting that the separation and parting between us would not be for long."

SIR ISAAC NEWTON

Our Ignorance Is Atlantic!

You, Sir Isaac Newton, are the only English scientist whose grave I had the opportunity to see when I visited Westminster Abbey.

My first acquaintance with you, Sir Isaac, came many years ago when I studied physics at St. Louis University. I was overwhelmed at times by the complexity of the ingenious mathematical system you created which is known as differential and integral calculus. I was thrilled to learn how you explained the mystery of the tides, founded the science of optics, and gave the world the law of universal gravitation and the three laws of motion that now bear your name.

The one thing that impressed me most about you, Newton, is your humility. In your day you were acclaimed the greatest scientist on the face of the earth. Honors flowed in upon you from every side, and yet, of yourself, you said: "I do not know what I may appear to the world, but to myself I seem to have been like a boy playing on the seashore...now and then finding a smoother pebble or a prettier shell than ordinary, while the great ocean of truth lay all undiscovered before me."

What impresses me today, Newton, some three centuries later, is that many of the world's outstanding scientists are equally honest in professing their humility.

During a commencement address which he delivered at St. Louis University, the late Dr. Wernher von Braun said, "Nature around us still harbors many thousand times more unsolved than solved mysteries."

Thomas Alva Edison was even more to the point: "We don't know one millionth of one percent about anything!"

In a fascinating article on gravity in *Space Digest*, Hal Hellman says, "We not only haven't been able to put gravity to work, but still don't know what it is. Newton, himself, never claimed to have explained its nature, only its behavior. Why have the secrets of gravitation remained so stubbornly locked up?"

In his excellent article in *Science World*, Simon Dresner points out: "No one is really sure what gravity is. In the latter part of his life, Einstein tried to show that gravity, electricity, and magnetism were all parts of one universal law, but he did not complete his work."

A few years ago Jacques Piccard made a voyage for one month in the experimental submarine, *Ben Franklin*, in the Gulf Stream, that great "river in the Atlantic Ocean" that flows north from the Gulf of Mexico.

Hundreds of feet below the surface of the Atlantic Ocean the *Ben Franklin*, with six men aboard, drifted silently northward with the flow of the Gulf Stream, from Florida to Massachusetts. With its engines cut off, the *Ben Franklin* moved with the current without rising to the surface. From viewing windows man got a new look at the mysterious ocean.

After the voyage Mr. Piccard said, "The Gulf Stream has been deeply studied and a few secrets have been uncovered." But he added that it will probably always hide most of its mysteries from man.

According to Mr. Piccard, the more you study science, the more mysteries you find. Like a great ocean, the mysteries seem to stretch out in all directions.

Dr. Ira M. Freeman, Professor of Physics at Rutgers University tells us that "physics is a purely experiential science and if it is asked *why* something is true, it can only answer that this is required by natural law. The falling of a stone can be attributed to gravitation, but it makes no sense to ask further how this force of attraction comes about because the laws of nature themselves cannot be explained except insofar as they can be referred to more general laws. However, there is an ultimate end to this process of referring back, and, when it is reached, science is at the boundaries of explanation. The laws of nature remain inexplicable."

At a Science Symposium held at the University of Wisconsin, Dr. Milton O. Pella, Professor of Science Education at the university pointed out again and again, "There is now more unknown than known."

A renowned neurosurgeon, Dr. Robert White, asks, "What is intelligence? We are light years away from knowing what intelligence is. We can try to define it with comparisons: we cannot say what it consists of. In a scientific laboratory, you'll never discover why one person can write so well or paint so well or do mathematics so well, and another cannot."

After our astronauts returned from the moon, Albert Rosenfeld wrote a fascinating article entitled, "Beyond the Moon—Discoveries—and More Mysteries." Mr. Rosenfeld tells us that "the news from beyond pointed up for man how truly enigmatic the universe remains in the face of his exciting efforts to fathom it.

"Man might well quail with humility and a sense of profound insignificance as he looks out at the unimaginable immensities of the cosmos."

Dr. James A. Van Allen is the famed scientist who discovered the Van Allen Radiation Belts that surround the earth, and which were named in his honor. "At the frontier of science," says Dr. Van Allen, "the effort is subjective, intuitive, controversial, sometimes courageous, often misdirected, often inconclusive, often plain wrong.

"It is anything but exact.

"There are no authoritative proclamations in science. The terms *conjecture*, *assumption*, and *presumption* are common ones."

At the convocation commemorating the 125th anniversary of the founding of the University of Notre Dame, Lee A. DuBridge reminded his distinguished audience of the limitation of human knowledge, not only in science, but in other fields as well.

Lee A. DuBridge has the experience that enables him to speak with authority. He is President of the California Institute of Technology, the institution which manages the world-famous Jet Propulsion Laboratory for the National Aeronautics and Space Administration.

"I could easily spend fifty years studying about the universe," said Lee DuBridge, "and still not know all I'd like to know.

"Why?

"For one simple reason: If I really were intent on learning all there was to know about physics, for example, or astronomy, or biology, or economics, or philosophy, I would soon come to some question for which *nobody had any answers*.

"How many elementary particles are there? *Nobody knows*.

"How does the DNA molecule govern the development of a newborn creature? *No one fully knows*. Why do men and nations always fight each other?

"We don't know!"

A number of years ago when I was visiting my parents in Omaha, Nebraska, I took time out to paint the white picket fence that ran on the east side of their yard. Alas, the fence was embraced by hundreds of morning glories, which I had to pull off before trying to paint. As I pulled off vine after vine, I discovered a strange thing: each vine twisted itself around the wooden slats in a counterclockwise fashion. I was intrigued. Not once did I find a rebellious vine that decided not to "follow the crowd."

About this time in my reading, I came across an amazing set of facts. In the northern hemisphere not only do vines generally twist themselves around their supports in a counterclockwise direction, but water whirlpooling down the drain of the kitchen sink spins in the same direction, and smoke rising from a chimney on a quiet day twists upward in the same counterclockwise fashion. In the southern hemisphere, the twist is reversed.

A few years after discovering this amazing set of facts, I had the unique good luck of being given a trip to Australia. I found myself in the Land Down Under. Once in my room at the hotel, with eager anticipation I filled the sink with water, and then pulled the plug. I watched with amazement. Yes! Indeed! The water in the sink did go down the drain in a spin *opposite* to that which it has in the northern hemisphere. For the first time in my life I watched water disappear in a clockwise twist.

In his fascinating book, *This Hill, This Valley*, Hal Borland says, "There are laws of nature that I doubt we shall ever understand.

"It is all very well to say that the twisting of vines and the whirling of water is the result of the turning of the earth.

"It even lends a kind of reasonable air," continues Hal Borland, "to say that in the southern hemisphere the twist is usually in the opposite direction.

"These are facts, not ultimate answers. That is the way things happen, not why they happen.

"Is a wild morning glory aware of the turning of the earth? Is a pole bean so endowed with this knowledge that I cannot force it to twist the other way?

"There is some law beyond, some way of life, some necessity of nature that I can recognize but not wholly understand."

Imagine my delight, Sir Isaac Newton, when one Christmas I was given a copy of a new publication called *The Encyclopaedia of Ignorance*. The very first sentence of the Editorial Preface reads: "Compared to the pond of knowledge, our ignorance remains atlantic. Indeed the horizon of the unknown recedes as we approach it."

To prove their point the authors Ronald Duncan and Miranda Weston-Smith enlisted 58 scientists to discuss what was unknown in their fields. The co-editors quickly discovered that "the more eminent they were, the more ready to run to us with their ignorance."

Some of the contributing scientists are, indeed, eminent: molecular biologists Francis Crick and Sir John Kendrew, chemist Linus Pauling (all Nobel laureates), anthropologist Donald Johanson, astronomers Sir Hermann Bondi and Thomas Gold, physicist John Wheeler. Some of the riddles they pose are: How did the universe come into being? How are galaxies formed? What causes pain? How does gravity work? How did humans evolve? How do birds navigate?

Great discoveries seem merely to have led to greater questions. For instance, Francis Crick won his Nobel Prize (with James D. Watson) for proposing the model for the double-helical structure of the master life molecule DNA. This explained how genetic material duplicates itself, and is considered the most important single development in 20th century biology.

Crick says, "We understand how an organism can build molecules, although the largest of them is far too minute for us to see, even with a high-powered microscope; yet we do not understand how it builds a flower or a hand or an eye, all of which are plainly visible to us." Even less is known, Crick notes, about how an animal's nervous system is formed, how the growth of the nerves is directed and how they are hooked up.

Physiologists Henry Buchtelk and Giovanni Berlucchi recall the question, "Where or how does the brain store its memories? That is the great mystery." And it remains unanswered.

Psychologist Wilse Webb admits that after years of research on sleep, he still does not understand its purpose.

Ignorance abounds in the physical sciences as well. Astronomer Douglas Gough points out that the inner structure, composition and workings of the sun, let alone distant stars, remain a mystery and that even sunspots, which were recorded by the ancient Chinese, still defy understanding.

For the past thirty years, Newton, I have led a dual role as priest-teacher at Campion High School, Prairie du Chien, Wisconsin. From Monday morning until late Friday afternoon my days were taken up teaching science. Outside of class hours I was in charge of the senior students in their dormitory building, Marquette Hall. On Saturday afternoon and Sunday morning I did parish work at St. John's Church in Prairie du Chien. On some weekends I also helped out in surrounding towns.

My background in science helps me approach the most agonizing and puzzling mystery of all, "Why does God allow suffering?"

The best answer I know comes from Nobel Prize winner, Dr. Charles H. Townes, the distinguished scientist whose work led to the laser beam we hear so much about today.

In a superb article he wrote concerning science and religion, Dr. Townes mentions that in the physical world we are surrounded by mysteries, and, therefore, it should come as no surprise to find that in the spiritual world, as well, we find mysteries.

"We know," said Dr. Townes, "that the most sophisticated present scientific theories, including modern quantum mechanics, are still incomplete.**

"We use them because in certain areas they are so amazingly right. Yet they lead us at times into inconsistencies which we do not understand, and where we must recognize that we have missed some crucial ideas.

"We simply admit and accept the paradoxes and hope that sometime in the future they will be resolved by a more complete understanding.

"We must expect paradoxes, and not be surprised or unduly troubled by them. We know of paradoxes in physics such as that concerning the nature of light, which have been resolved by deeper understanding. We know of some which are still unresolved.

"In the realm of religion, we are troubled by the suffering around us, and its apparent inconsistency with a God of love.

"Such paradoxes do not destroy our faith. They simply remind us of a limited understanding, and at times provide a key to learning more."

Dr. Lewis Thomas is president and chief executive officer of the Memorial Sloan-Kettering Cancer Center in New York City. He is a biologist, a researcher, published poet, and famous author. A collection of 29 of his essays was published under the title, *The Lives of a Cell: Notes of a Biology Watcher.* The book proved to be a best seller and has been translated into eleven languages.

In another book, *The Medusa and the Snail*, Dr. Thomas says, "The only solid piece of scientific truth about which I feel totally confident is that we are profoundly ignorant about nature: I regard this as the major discovery of the past hundred years of biology."

Dr. Thomas goes on to say that it would have amazed the brightest minds of the eighteenth-century Enlightenment to be told by any of us today how little we know, and how bewildering seems the way ahead.

"It is a sudden confrontation," says Dr. Thomas, "with the depth and scope of ignorance that represents the most significant contribution of twentieth-century science to the human intellect."

To those who are perplexed with doubts about their faith, Pope John Paul I said, "Don't fling away your faith! Ten thousand difficulties, Newman said, do not make a doubt. Remember this: a sense of mystery is necessary to man. We don't know everything about anything, Pascal said. I know many things about myself but not everything.

"I don't know exactly what my life is, or my intelligence. How can I expect to understand and know everything about God?"

I deem it proper, Newton, to conclude this chapter with the words of an unknown author, "All that we have seen should teach us to trust the Creator for what we have not seen."

SIR WALTER SCOTT

Ideals That Light Stars

I made my first acquaintance with you, Sir Walter Scott, in high school. Our first assignment in freshman English was to memorize the first twenty lines of your captivating poem, *The Lady of the Lake*.

The assignment paid off. To this day I catch snatches of those lines ringing through my memory, like nuances of bells indicating subtle passages in music.

I was fascinated by two things, Sir Walter: the story of your life, and the inspiration from your poems and novels. What impressed me most of all is that the inspiration of your words was backed up by the example of your own life. You practiced what you preached.

In the winter of 1773, when you were eighteen months old, you were afflicted with an illness that left you with a withered leg. During the years that followed, you were so sick, you missed much school. Left to your own resources you discovered the truth given to us by Cicero centuries before. Books are among our best companions. Books are doors to wide, new worlds. You turned to reading about Scotland's past. Not content to learn from books alone, you de-cided to learn still more about the ballads and legends of the Highland clans by rambling around the country collecting its folklore and studying its landscape.

To please your parents, you took up the study of law, and were admitted to the bar, but your practice of law remained secondary to your love of literature.

Single-handed you undertook the incredible task of unraveling the past of six centuries, and amazed the world with your results. You became the founder of the modern historical novel. You were called by Alfred Lord Tennyson, "the greatest man of letters of the nineteenth century."

Your first important work, the fine collection of Scotch ballads and legends known as *The Minstrelsy of the Scottish Border*, was proof of the value of your early reading and your trips around the country. Your poems and novels are filled with optimism, action and truth. Honor and heroism—two qualities that you glorified in your writings—were exemplified in your life.

In 1826, a publishing firm in which you were a partner threw you into debt to the extent of 60,000 pounds. You could have escaped the obligation by declaring bankruptcy, and thus continued your gracious style of living as a country gentleman. Instead, you gave up your beautiful home in Abbotsford, and took lodgings in Edinburgh where you worked feverishly writing novels to pay the creditors. Seven years of unending work ruined your health and led you to your grave. You died rather than besmirch your honor.

John Hay said of you, "Scott owes his enduring masterhood to his mentality and morality. Valor, purity, loyalty, these are the essential and undying elements of the charm with which this great magician has soothed and lulled the weariness of the world for three tormented generations."

I find it very worthy of note, Sir Walter, that the first important fee you obtained from your writings was used to purchase a silver candlestick for your mother.

According to J. L. Stoddard, you, Sir Walter, were "one whom Nature framed to bear the grand old name of gentleman."

Like most writers of great literature, you were a man to whom life was a great adventure. It has been said of your poems, Sir Walter, that "they contain more of the Homeric or epic element than any other poems in the English language."

Few men, Sir Walter, who battle for the right, battle for it with the calm fortitude, the cheerful equanimity, with which you battled. You stand high among those "who, ever with a frolic welcome, took the thunder and the sunshine and opposed free hearts, free foreheads."

You are among those who have been able to display "One equal temper of heroic hearts, made weak by time and fate, but strong in will to strive, to seek, to find, and not to yield."

You, Sir Walter, will continue to be read as long as people appreciate the spontaneous outpourings of a genius who writes with all the ease and joyousness with which the blackbird sings. There is about your writings the freshness of the morning dew. Your poetry and prose are fired with your own courage and animation; they are fired with your inspiration and your high sense of honor. They reflect your good cheer, and your admiration for chivalry when knighthood was in flower.

It was at nine a.m. on the morning of May 16, 1826, Sir Walter, that your cherished wife died. Two days later you wrote that, although her body had been laid to rest in Cryburgh cemetery, she, herself, still lived. "She is sentient and conscious of my emotions somewhere—somehow; how we cannot tell; yet I would not this moment renounce the mysterious yet certain hope that I shall see her in a better world, for all that this world can give me."

As the sun began to set on your own life, Sir Walter, you wrote: "I am drawing to the close of my career. I have been, perhaps, the most voluminous author of the day, and it is a comfort to me to think that I have tried to unsettle no man's faith, to corrupt no man's principles, that I have written nothing which I should wish blotted."

In chapter four of this book, Sir Walter, I talked with Cicero concerning the magic of words, and the advantages that come from reading good books. Now, I'd like to discuss with you how poetry comforts, gives encouragement, and lights stars in our skies to serve as ideals.

During all the years I've been giving sermons, I find that when I quote poetry, the eyes of the people sparkle like newly minted dimes. Poems attract attention like magnets attract steel. Once, after I had said an early Mass, a woman came up to let me know how touched she was by the poem I quoted in my sermon. The poem was "I see His Blood upon the Rose" by Joseph Mary Plunkett:*

I see his blood upon the rose
And in the stars the glory of his eyes,
His body gleams amid eternal snows,
His tears fall from the skies.

I see his face in every flower;
The thunder and the singing of the birds
Are but his voice—and carven by his power
Rocks are his written words.

All pathways by his feet are worn,
His strong heart stirs the ever-beating sea,
His crown of thorns is twined with every thorn,
His cross is every tree.

In private conversations I discover that many people who often find themselves lost in a string of "Blue Mondays" or wandering in a bleak desert of loneliness often find consolation and help in poems. Why? Among other things, poetry shows a person that he or she is not alone. Others have experienced the same feelings. No man is an island. By means of poetry we link hands across the seas of loneliness to share our lives with others.

According to Dr. J. J. Leedy, poetry helps people develop an optimistic philosophy of life and inspires them to constructive action. Poetry helps people explore their feelings and face life's problems.

It is interesting to note that the poems of Stevenson, Longfellow, Shakespeare, Wordsworth, Emerson, Keats, Shelley, Frost, and Sandburg are among the most effective for the rehabilitation of mental patients. Poems such as Coleridge's "The Rime of the Ancient Mariner," Keat's "La Belle Dame sans Merci," Longfellow's "Evangeline," Poe's "Annabelle Lee," and Shelley's "The Indian Serenade," seem to exert an almost hypnotic effect on the patients. Poetry is magic, a transfiguration of words, a combination of sounds that awakens something within us. Poets use words to fence in a fragment of the world, wherein mental images, like the acrobats in a circus, joyously swing through the air. Just as a king is clad in a regal mantle, so must truth be clad in beauty. A few metaphors, like jewels, add warmth and luster to cold bare facts.

A poet helps us to see things the way they should be, that is, the way we saw them when we looked at them with a child's eyes in all that hidden splendor which turns life into a bazaar of wonders.

In the company of great poets, such as yourself, Sir Walter, one feels to be in the company of giants whose torches keep on lighting candles in the dark corners that inevitably spring up in every life.

It has been said that human life, like the soldier's in war, consists of long periods of tedious waiting interpolated between brief moments of intense dramatic action. Poetry liberates us from the daily commonplace, the anxieties, and the problems that are timeless realities of the universe.

Perhaps the best definition of a poet is one who is amazed by everything and beautifully sings his amazement. The poet possesses a magic loom of words on which he weaves tremendous possibilities.

Just as the sculptor infuses spirit into his clay, so do some poets give their poetry a music superior to that of simple metric rhyme. The true poet is possessed of that mysterious power everybody feels and that no philosopher can explain. A poet crystallizes the exploration of his inner self into verse. He is the man of profundities, and he will speak in a voice that resounds through the caverns of the cosmic. He captures dreams by the handful. Some dreams, like slippery fish, slip through his fingers; with others, he weaves the mesh of his poetry. His dreams reveal the cravings of his soul in poems that pierce his heart like a sword.

The sign of a great poet is to tell something that no one else has told, yet something that is not new to us. It means to awaken the poetry we all have within us. It is a message cast into the sea in a bottle.

Good poetry smiles or it sobs, it winks, it jumps, it lights a bright candle. A good poem is like a giant wave that picks you up like a surf board and lifts you to the stars.

In the magic words of a poem some hear the tread of ancient folklore, some the beat of the sea, the passion of the gale, and some hear the voice of some soaring thing that will not stay imprisoned.

No wonder that Everett W. Hill informs us: "I love the sounds of forest drums, of violin strings and tones of reeds. Crashing cymbals of a storm seem at times to fit my needs."

In his "Apostrophe to the Ocean," Lord Byron says:*

There is a pleasure in the pathless woods,
There is a rapture on the lonely shore,
There is society, where none intrudes,
By the deep sea, and music in its roar:
I love not Man the less, but Nature more,
From these our interviews, in which I steal
From all I may be, or have been before,

To mingle with the Universe, and feel
What I can ne'er express, yet cannot all conceal.

The song of the poet shall forever abide in the
heart of the world, and the winds, and the murmuring
tide. His words will gather thunder as they roll, and as
the lightning to the thunder which follows it, illumi-
nating the mind of man and making all wonder.

A great poem can hold and fix the most fleeting of
all things—the experience of the emotions, as a flash
of lightning in the night stops the sliding of a river.

A great poem can suddenly fill a fugitive moment
with warmth and laughter. It can provide great swing-
ing words for our dreams to live by. With his scroll a
poet can shake the world.

The poet Alfred Tennyson tells us:*

I am a part of all that I have met;
Yet all experience is an arch where through
Gleams that untraveled world whose margin fades
Forever and forever when I move.
How dull it is to pause, to make an end,
To rust unburnished, not to shine in use!
As though to breathe were life!

When the hand of death reaches out to take our
loved ones from us, we find consolation in these
words of a poet whose name I cannot find:

Fast as the rolling seasons bring
    The hour of fate to those we love,
Each pearl that leaves the broken string
    Is set in Friendship's crown above.
As narrower grows the earthly chain,
    The circle widens in the sky;

These are our treasures that remain,
　But those are stars that beam on high.

A poet worthy of the name is an artist who imitates God, the Creator of all, because with his talents and through his works he brings harmony, beauty, and nobility into men's lives. Thus the poet invites us to contemplate the unseen and unheard through what is seen and heard.

A poem that is a work of art can exert a vast influence, whether it be with respect to the growth and unfolding of human personality, or the development of civil society, or the mutual union of men, a union that paves the way to union with God. Poetry provides a special pathway to the human heart.

Using words for brush strokes, poets paint "images" or mental pictures. According to Father Daniel L. Flaherty, S.J., "Images have a more immediate and profound effect on the way we think and act than do documents (for all the light and learned arguments they provide our intellects) or exhortations.

"Images capture the imagination—possibly the most powerful, if irrational, motivating force in man—through some sort of near magical shorthand of the mind and will."

A poet deals with love, hope, faith and trust, the unseen things that people feel, which are far greater than the material things some people collect and mistake for real.

In this mood Deanna K. Edwards wrote:

All the warm and tender feelings
That were born the day we met
Still live on and grow within me,
Much too precious to forget.

The song of a poet is sometimes like that of a bird in spring. It begins as a solitary, cautious staccato, then builds up into a vibrant, pulsing clamor, and, finally, erupts into a concerto of strident insistence, testimony to the indisputable wonder of a morning in May.

It is interesting to note, Sir Walter, that when you were a boy, you were considered dull in school. You often were made to stand in the dunce corner with the high pointed hat of shame on your head. You were approximately twelve years old when you happened to be in a home where some famous literary guests were entertained.

Robert Burns, the Scottish poet, was standing admiring a picture under which was written the couplet of a stanza. Burns inquired concerning the author of the couplet. No one seemed to know. Finally, you made your way up to his side, named the author, and quoted the rest of the poem.

Burns was surprised and delighted. Laying his hand on your head he exclaimed, "Ah, bairnie, ye will be a great man in Scotland some day." And from that day on, Sir Walter, you were a changed lad. One sentence of encouragement set you on the road to greatness.

Philip James Bailey would have us keep in mind that we live in deeds, not years; in thoughts, not breaths; in feelings, not in figures on a dial. We should count life by heart throbs. He most lives who thinks most, feels the noblest, acts the best.

William Wordsworth urges us to let our mind be a mansion for all lovely forms. "Thy memory be as a dwelling-place for all sweet sounds and harmonies."

If we are noble, then the nobleness that lies in other men, sleeping, but never dead, will rise in majesty to meet our own.

Henry David Thoreau put his prayer into poetry:

Great God, I ask Thee for no meaner pelf
Than that I may not disappoint myself,
That in my action I may soar as high
As I can now discern with this clear eye.

St. Paul tells us to "be transformed by the renewing of your mind" (Romans 12:2). What better way to renew our minds than by taking to heart the inspiring words from an anonymous poet:

Take time to laugh
It is the music of the soul.

Take time to think
It is the source of power.

Take time to play
It is the source of perpetual youth.

Take time to read
It is the fountain of wisdom.

Take time to pray
It is the greatest power on earth.

Take time to love and be loved
It is a God-given privilege.

Take time to be friendly
It is the road to happiness.

I would like to conclude this chapter, Sir Walter, by recalling the most dramatic example I know concerning the power of a poem to bring inspiration, hope and comfort.

Since the example involves Mr. Bernard A. Kennedy, I will have to first give you a little of his background.

When I was a sophomore in high school, I met Mr. Kennedy's son, Bernard, Jr., who was one of my classmates. It was through him that I was introduced to the Kennedy family.

When I was a junior, the Kennedy family moved to Prairie du Chien, Wisconsin, where Mr. Kennedy was offered the job of principal of Prairie du Chien High School. So successful was Mr. Kennedy as principal that he held this position for thirty-two years, until advancing years forced him to retire.

When I was sent to Campion High School in Prairie du Chien I established contact with the Kennedy family.

As the years slipped away over the Wisconsin hills, the Kennedy children grew up, married, and moved out into other cities and towns. Only Mr. and Mrs. Kennedy were left in Prairie du Chien.

When Mrs. Kennedy preceded Mr. Kennedy in death, it was an experience that put Mr. Kennedy's faith to the test. They had loved each other with a total, all-abiding love. Their marriage was one in which two lives had truly become one, and this oneness grew with the swiftly passing years. Their married life was of that type once described by Archbishop Fulton J. Sheen: "In true married love it is not so much that two hearts walk side by side through life. Rather two hearts become one heart. That is why death is not a separation of two hearts, but rather the tearing apart of one heart. It is this that makes the bitterness of grief."

Since Mr. Kennedy was now living by himself, I tried to arrange my schedule so that once about every two weeks I could stop in to visit with him in the evening. Almost invariably his conversation would drift around to describing his great loss, and how he missed his dear wife.

Why did God keep him waiting so long on earth, when the one thing he wanted most of all was to be with his dear wife?

How many years must he endure this solitude?

It was truly inspiring and deeply moving to listen to Mr. Kennedy describe his love for his beloved wife. I wish that all young people could have listened to this white-haired grandfather describe what true love really is.

Mr. Kennedy went to Mass every day of the week. On Sunday morning he attended the 11:30 a.m. Mass, which was the Mass that I said at St. John's Church for many, many years.

One Sunday, during my sermon on death, I quoted the following lines from the poet Henry King:

> But hark! My pulse like a soft drum
> Beats my approach, tells Thee I come;
> And slow howe'er my marches be,
> I shall at last sit down by Thee.

Mr. Kennedy was sitting in the second pew, and when I quoted the above lines his face lit up with a beatific smile. He remained in church after Mass so that he could inform me how the words of this poem rang like a bell in his memory, and echoed refrains of love and contentment.

Thereafter, on my visits to his lovely home, Mr. Kennedy told me time and time again how much inspiration and insight he gained from this poem.

As I look back, it seems like only a short span of years until God called Mr. Kennedy home. On that happy day of his death, the marches were over for B. A. Kennedy. At last he sat down in joy and happiness with his beloved wife.

FR. FRANCIS J. FINN, s.j.

Friend of Youth

When I was a young boy in Butte, Montana, I had the wonderful delight, Father Finn, of reading many of your fascinating books such as *Tom Playfair, Percy Wynn, Harry Dee, Cupid of Campion, Claude Lightfoot,* and *His First and Last Appearance.*

At that time, in the early 1920's, the mere mention of your name conjured up visions of a magic pen that went racing across the page spinning a magic web of words to capture and hold young minds. Alas, you, yourself, remained a shadowy figure. The lightning flashes from your mind illuminated the printed page, but you, as a person, remained unknown to me.

And thus things remained until I was stationed at Creighton University in Omaha, Nebraska. One January I received a letter from my friend, Father William Barnaby Faherty, S.J., Director of the Saint Stanislaus Seminary Museum, Florissant, Missouri. Fr. Faherty was inviting me to take part in a conference on the history of the seminary. The distinguished alumnus assigned to me was none other than you, Father Finn.

I checked the Creighton University Library, but it had no reference material on you. Then I phoned the public library. The girl at the information desk informed me that they had one copy of *Father Finn, the Story of His Life Told by Himself.*

I was delighted, but I did not walk down to the public library that day. January of that year was the coldest in the 118 year history of the Omaha weather bureau. With sub-zero temperatures plus winds that drove the chill index down to sixty below zero, I decided to wait until the first mild day before walking the mile and a half to the public library.

At last, the mercury made bold enough to creep into the mid 20's, and so, I went downtown to pick up the copy of the story of your life.

That evening, when I opened your book and began to read, I was fascinated. Now, for the first time, I was about to learn the background behind your writing, and the conditions under which you produced so many captivating books.

It was on October 4, 1859, in St. Louis, Missouri, that you opened your eyes to the wonders of God's world. One of the outstanding memories of your early years was one of your grandfather. He had just finished reading *Dombey and Son* by Charles Dickens. As he finished the last sentence and closed the book, he rose and said, "This is the finest book I have ever read in my life."

The impression made upon you was extraordinary. "What a wonderful book," you thought. "Why grandfather has been reading books all his life. If that is the most remarkable book he ever read, it must be a very remarkable book indeed."

You could not read at that time; but, through all the years that followed, you carried in your head the memory of *Dombey and Son* and a high idea of Charles Dickens.

I had to smile, Father Finn, when I read your reference to Omaha. "My simple home life was broken in these days by a visit to Omaha. I think I must have spent a month with my father and mother in that then semi-civilized town." You mentioned that you were delighted "with the spectacle of indians and squaws roaming the streets in their native costumes."

At last came the day when you learned to read. About the same time came a period of sickness, and so, you buried yourself in what books you could get. One of these books was *Fabiola* by Cardinal Wiseman. The beautiful story of those early Christian martyrs had a profound influence upon your life. Religion began to mean something to you. No wonder you wrote, "Since the day of reading *Fabiola*, I have carried the conviction that one of the greatest things in the world is to get the right book into the hands of the right boy or girl."

From the day you picked up *Fabiola* you became a ravenous reader. You mention that your power of absorption was so intense when you became interested in a book, there might be conversation, music and all sorts of things going on about you, but your mind was far away sailing on the magic ocean of fantasy. Many a time you were addressed by your mother or father without being brought back to reality. They had to shout at you, or shake you to drag you out of the realms of fairyland.

You were about eleven when you discovered Charles Dickens, a discovery led up to, no doubt, by the unforgettable remark of your grandfather concerning *Dombey and Son*.

You wrote, "I began with *Nicholas Nichleby*. Oh, how I loved that book! I must have read it, between the ages of eleven and seventeen, at least a dozen times. Next to *Nicholas Nickleby* in my affections came the *Pickwick Papers.*"

When you were in high school you discovered Washington Irving, Prescott, Cooper, and others. Then came Shakespeare, and you read and saw *Hamlet*, *Othello*, and *King Lear.*

In 1877, you went to Saint Stanislaus Seminary at Florissant, Missouri, and entered the Order of the Society of Jesus. I was intrigued, Father Finn, by your frank confession of two things you missed in the seminary: "I was constantly diving into my pockets, only to remember that I no longer carried cigarette paper and tobacco. With the putting on of the cassock the cigarette was cast away. After about four years of cigarette smoking, the deprivation of it was really a hardship.

"There was another little thing which I really felt. Since the age of twelve I had played the violin. I had come to have a great love for the instrument. Always, after coming back from school, I took up my instrument and played it for an hour or more with great pleasure."

Because of ill health, you were not able to finish your four consecutive years at Florissant. After three and one half years, you were sent to teach boys at St. Mary's College, St. Mary's, Kansas.

It is indicative of your character, Father Finn, that you wrote of this transfer to Saint Mary's College: "I considered myself very rich in my equipment. I had brought with me a fine copy of *Bryant's Household Book of Poetry*, a present from my mother when I left St. Louis. In those days poetry meant much to me."

The more I read about the lives of people who write, Father Finn, the more I discover that their writing is often the result of two things: their *literary background* or reading, and their *own experience*.

In particular, Father Finn, I find an interesting comparison between your life and that of Sir Walter Scott. Both of you as boys were sick, and both of you turned to reading. After reading about Scotland's past, Scott obtained his actual experience by rambling around the country collecting its folklore and studying its landscape. After you absorbed the literary output of Dickens and other greats in the English language, you obtained your experience as a teacher and prefect of the boys at Saint Mary's College.

As I read of your first experience with boys, Father Finn, I was struck with the realization that—even though I'm more than half a century behind you—my first experience with boys was similar to yours in many respects.

You were assigned to a boarding school, and so was I. Almost sixty years after you took the Union Pacific train from the Union Depot in Kansas City, Missouri, for Saint Mary's, Kansas, I took the Chicago and Northwestern train from the Union Depot in Omaha, Nebraska, for Rushville, Nebraska. There a handsome young man by the name of Bill Thomas met me with a truck loaded with freight and drove me the last thirty miles to Holy Rosary Mission, Pine Ridge, South Dakota.

Like you, "I was with the boys from early morning until I went to bed at night towards ten o'clock." I was in charge of approximately one hundred boys in a huge dormitory on the third floor of Red Cloud Hall. We were so crowded for room that the foot of one cot was placed against the head of the next cot. The aisles between the rows of cots were only about 18 inches wide. I slept in the southeast corner of this huge dormitory.

Each member of the Jesuit Community (priests and brothers) had to rise at 5:00 a.m. and prepare for the community Mass at 5:30 a.m., followed by prayer and meditation.

At 6:30 a.m. I returned to the dormitory to get the boys out of bed. Since we had no electric bells, I simply gave a blast on a police whistle to jerk the boys back to reality. I had to have all the boys out of the dormitory at 6:55 so they would be on time for the student Mass at 7:00 a.m.

While another Jesuit, Hal Fuller, was in charge of the boys during Mass, I ate my breakfast. I returned to the chapel in time to escort the boys from Mass to the dining hall, where I monitored them while they ate.

From 8:30 until noon I taught 30 boys in the same classroom. Then came lunch. At 1:00 p.m. I was back in the same classroom with the same junior high boys until 3:30 p.m.

From 3:30 to 5:00 I helped to supervise the boys on the playing fields, or during the winter months, in the gym or playroom. From 5:00 to 6:00 I was back in the same classroom with the same boys for study time. Then came supper. From 7:00 to 8:30 I was again in the classroom with the same boys for more study. This was followed by evening recreation, which, again, I helped to supervise.

At 8:45 p.m. the smaller boys, those in the first four years of grade school, went to bed. Since I was in charge of the older grade school boys and high school boys, I had to supervise them at their recreation until

9:30 p.m. At this time they walked up the concrete steps to the dormitory on the top floor and, in complete silence, prepared for bed.

I would stand in the middle of the dorm until all the students were in bed, then I'd turn out the main lights, and leave only the night lights burning. I'd remain standing in the middle of the dormitory until I could tell by the sounds of breathing that all the students were asleep. At 10:00 p.m. I took off for dreamland myself.

You know now, Father Finn, why I agree 100% with you when you said, "One of the difficulties of those days was to keep the boys busy in the hours of recreation. There was no trouble in the autumn or in the springtime; but the long and dreary winter had its difficulties."

And I had the "Blue Mondays" of which you said, "When I entered the classroom of a morning, I entered with that same wish, that it were supper time and all were well."

I did have one advantage, Father Finn, which you did not have. You came to St. Mary's before the coming of Hollywood and the silver screen. When I came to the Sioux Indians at Holy Rosary Mission, the one big thing all the students looked forward to each weekend was a movie.

It was my job to run the 35mm projectors in the movie booth located on the east balcony of the gym. On Saturday night the film was shown to all the boys and girls at the Mission. (We Jesuits were in charge of the 210 boys from first grade through high school. The Sisters of Saint Francis were in charge of the 220 girls.)

On Sunday night the film was shown to all those who lived near the Mission. In those days, in the late '30's, many Sioux still traveled via wagon or horseback. On Sunday night the area in front of the gym, a wide sandy stretch of ground, looked like a lot for a Hollywood western. Teams and wagons were everywhere. The barb wire fence on the east side of the area served as a hitching rail for the saddle horses.

The two most popular stars among the Sioux in those days were Gene Autry and Roy Rogers. Whenever their pictures were shown, we could count on a full house.

Whatever the younger boys in the grade school saw taking place on the silver screen on Saturday night, they would imitate on the playground the following week. For many days after the showing of the motion picture *Beau Geste*, the young boys broke up into two groups. One group represented Gary Cooper, Ray Milland, Robert Preston and the French Foreign Legion besieged at Fort Zinderneuf, under the brutal Sergeant Markoff (Brian Donlevy). The other group represented the horde of Touaregs, the wild desert tribe, which attacked the fort.

Day after day the "Touaregs" would be driven back by the "Legionnaires" who repelled the invaders by heaving "dust bombs" over their heads. To make a "dust bomb" the boys would spread out their wide, big red handkerchiefs on the ground, scoop up sand and dust with their hands and place the mound of dust in the center of the handkerchief. The boys would then pick up the four ends of the handkerchief and hold the ends between the fingers of their right hand while they hurled the "bomb" around their heads a couple of times to pick up speed, and then let go.

Because I was teaching Sioux Indians who ranked among the poorest of the poor, the Mission gave the boys everything they needed, though at times the items might not be what you would expect.

Take the matter of a mattress. At the start of the school year each student was given a canvas sack as long as he was tall. The canvas sacks were brought to the hay stack in back of the barn where the students stuffed them with straw. The sacks were then sewn shut. After a month or so of use, each mattress became form fitting, and I could tell by looking at it, just who slept there.

In order to get meat to feed the boys and girls in the Mission, the Jesuit Brothers, around the turn of the century, had taken up homesteads in Nebraska, some twelve miles away. The Mission Ranch, as it was called, was still helping to feed the students in my day. To my great delight I was able to spend my summers there working in the company of another Jesuit, Hal Fuller. In June we helped with the roundup and branding. Then came days of putting up fence and making hay. Every now and then I drove a truckload of cattle to the sales ring in Chadron, Nebraska. The best cattle were sold to help make money to defray the terrible expense of running Holy Rosary Mission. The poorer grade of cattle we kept for our own use. Every Thursday at Holy Rosary Mission was "butcher day." A giant of a man, genial Brother Henry Bauer, S.J., did the work required to keep meat on the table for all the students and faculty.

It is over forty years since I taught my first class at Holy Rosary Mission and yet the names of those boys in that class still echo in my memory, and no wonder. Here are but a few of the fascinating names: Joe Blue

Horse, George Stinking Bear, American Afraid of Horse, Edgar Pumpkin Seed, Howard Bad Milk, Joe Angel, Oliver Jumping Eagle, George Kills Enemy In Water, Leo She Elk Voice Walking, Clayton Jealous of Him, and David Crazy Thunder.

I remember the time Father Joseph Zimmerman, S.J., had a wedding Mass and put this question to the young couple: "Leroy Pumpkin Seed will you take Winona Shot To Pieces here present for your lawful wife?"

During the three years I taught at Holy Rosary Mission, I stayed there during the summer also, and worked at the Mission Ranch. When you taught at Saint Mary's College, Father Finn, you spent a few weeks of the summer at Beulah, Wisconsin. In the story of your life you mention, "After the year's hard work in the various colleges, Beulah Island was awaiting the Jesuit teachers for a prolonged outing."

It was at Beulah that you entered upon the field of writing for the young. Your story "Charlie's Victory" was accepted by *The Sacred Heart Messenger.*

Following your vacation at Beulah, you were sent to Woodstock College to study philosophy. At the end of one year, however, your health was so bad, you were sent back to Saint Mary's to teach.

One afternoon while you were sitting at the teacher's desk supervising the boys in your classroom, who were busy writing a composition, the thought leaped into your head, "Why not write about such boys as they are before you in the flesh?"

Within your reach were a pad of paper and a pencil. You took them and started to write. Your pencil moved easily in those days, and in a few minutes you had written the first chapter of *Tom Playfair.*

It is fascinating to note that "nothing was further from my thought at the moment than writing for publication. That chapter was written for the boys in my class and for other boys who should come under my care in other years. I started this story with nothing else in my mind than to present, once and for all, my ideal of the typical American Catholic boy."

There were ten minutes remaining in the class day. The boys had finished their compositions, and so, you read the chapter to them then and there just as you had written it. The entire class listened with open ears and with an enthusiasm that left nothing to be desired.

It was then that you decided to furnish those boys with further chapters of *Tom Playfair*, and further incidents, real or possible, in a Catholic boarding school. You mention that in those days your imagination was lively. Your pencil never lacked for material. Never did you have to pause to think of what to write next. "In fact," you said, "my pencil raced over the paper in a futile endeavor to catch up with the incidents, adventures and fun which crowded my brain."

Strangest of all, "At no time during the forty or fifty days that I wrote did it occur to me that I was writing for the general public. No. I was writing for a boy audience."

In February, 1884, your health broke down and you were sent to Saint Louis, "a broken-down man, a failure and without anything to show but a thick bundle of manuscripts containing neither beginning, middle nor end, a series of adventures and episodes concerning my little friend Tom Playfair."

In September, 1884, you were sent to teach at St. Xavier's College in Cincinnati, Ohio, and the following year you returned to Woodstock to resume your broken course in philosophy. During your second year at Woodstock you began writing and publishing stories for children once more. One of the striking episodes from the story of *Tom Playfair* appeared in the *Youth's Companion.*

The following year, when you were teaching at Marquette College in Milwaukee, you brought out your first book, *Percy Wynn.* In August you went to your study of theology at Woodstock. Classes did not begin until September 11th. On September 1st there suddenly flashed upon your mind a happy thought. At once you seated yourself at your desk, took out pen and paper, and began writing your longest story, *Harry Dee.* You finished the story in ten days.

Concerning these ten days you wrote, "I was in the prime of life, thirty years of age, and charged with energy, and my pen hurried over the paper with an ease which, looking backward into those years, I cannot but marvel at. For ten days I must have averaged from eight thousand to nine thousand words a day. Also, I played handball, attended an outing, and did many other things that were in no wise concerned with the story of *Harry Dee.*"

By the end of your third year of theology you had three published volumes to your credit—*Percy Wynn*, *Harry Dee*, *Tom Playfair*, and another story, *Claude Lightfoot*, ready for the publisher.

Tom Playfair proved to be your most popular book. It was written for your boys in 1883, parts of it were published as episodes between 1883 and 1889. The book was finished in 1889.

"There was something in *Tom Playfair*," you wrote, "which, in the years that have followed, brought it to a position where, as I am credibly informed by my publishers, it is beyond question the most successful Catholic book written for boys and girls ever published in the English tongue."

Tom Playfair was hardly out in the English edition when it was translated into the German language, in which tongue it went through many editions. In 1908 the Portuguese version appeared; in 1910 the Italian; in 1913 the Polish; in 1925 the French, Flemish and Dutch.

It is interesting, Father Finn, to know that you had discovered the ideal conditions for your literary productivity. "To give my pen wings, all I needed was a vast leisure. At the end of a leisurely vacation I was able to write, almost in a single burst, the story of *Harry Dee*, and during the vacation that followed my first year of theology I wrote *Claude Lightfoot*."

You went on to say that when at the end of a hard day's class you sat down to write or revise, you found your pen difficult and your imagination barren. "I could not change or correct, much less create."

In 1928, when Father Daniel A. Lord, S.J., wrote the preface to the story of your life, he said that you, Father Finn, "pioneered in Catholic literature at a time when Catholic literature in the United States was at a dismally low ebb."

Throughout the story of your life, Father Finn, you are frank in admitting that you suffered now and then from one of the most terrible crosses of all—mental agony. Concerning your second year at Saint Mary's College, when you were in charge of a dormitory, you wrote: "I did a great deal of praying in the dormitory. I was suffering from mental distress. I knew that I was facing an ordeal. In those days I was going through my Gethsemane."

The "blues" hit you again during your first year in philosophy: "I did very little study until early spring. In fact I was fighting against depression, discouragement—the blues, and it was a hard fight. I remember that at various times I felt so despondent that I would lock my door, refuse all visitors and bury myself in a book."

Towards the end of your life you wrote: "From the early days of my noviceship to the present time I have always thought that if we cast our cares upon the Lord He will not fail us. Suffering again and again from extremely low spirits, which I later discovered were a part of my malady, I had always put my troubles in the hands of God. He never failed me."

One of the greatest tests of your spirit took place at Saint Mary's College when you met Father Kinsella, a most literary Jesuit, and, in the minds of many, the best critic in the province. You mentioned your dream of becoming a writer. He very kindly offered to look over your three manuscripts, and to give you a candid opinion.

In due time Father Kinsella called you to his room and pointed out defects galore in your manuscripts. He ended with the words: "And my advice to you, Fr. Finn, is to give up all idea of writing for publication. There is nothing in your work to show that you will ever make a writer."

You mentioned, Father Finn, that the most depressing month in a boarding school is February. I agree with you 100%! All my life teaching young people has been spent in boarding schools. By February the boys start to tire of ice skating and skiing. Worst of all is the intense cold. The wind becomes a wild wolf stalking the shivering countryside on paws of winter, running with ice upon his hide. Day after day howling winds drop the chill index to *sixty-five below zero* or more. Being outdoors becomes too uncomfortable, even for red-blooded young men. Result—the boys are confined with you inside the school buildings from morning to night, and then, on through the night until the same thing all over the next day!

This depressing effect of February is not limited to boarding school. The *Chicago Tribune* once had giant headlines that ran shouting across the top of the first page: "New Epidemic—The Blizzard Blues."

The article went on to say that Chicago's worst recorded winter (1978-1979) had created an epidemic of the blizzard blues. Hundreds of people had already cracked under the strain, and mental health experts feared many more would suffer emotional problems.

According to Dr. James L. Cavanaugh, clinical director of psychiatry at Rush-Presbyterian-St. Luke's Medical Center, "There is simply no end to it. The snow, ice, cold, traffic jams, commuting problems, and other stresses are just like the drops of water in the Chinese water torture. Eventually everyone reaches a breaking point."

The newspaper went on to say that many already had succumbed to the strain. They ranged from the snowplow driver who went berserk and plowed into cars, killing one person, to an increase in murders, and an upsurge in patients at psychiatrists' offices.

In the story of your life, Father Finn, you mention that there were long intervals when many years slipped past without a single book leaping from your pen. This lack of writing was due to the pressure of work and the debilitating effects of sickness.

Under such circumstances, Father Finn, no one would have blamed you for turning to the Lord in prayer and asking, "Why me, Lord? Certainly, Lord, You realize that I'm the Number One Writer of Catholic books for young people. If You let things run amuck, I won't be able to write the books that are so in demand. If only, Lord, You would remove suffering from my life, I could function much more efficiently."

Pain, however unwelcome, comes into everybody's life. It can range from dull distress to excruciating agony. Its cause may be clear—an injury or illness—or it may have no known cause. The only thing worse than pain in our own lives is pain and suffering in the lives of those we love. When the steel jaws of pain trap shut on those we love, their suffering becomes ours.

We would like so much to have a magic wand to encircle all our dreams for those we love, to remove all pain and suffering from their lives, and to make their dreams come true.

Alas, we often feel helpless as a person tied to a tree along the bank of a deep, swift-flowing river. We are forced to watch helplessly while those we love struggle in the dark, swirling waters. No wonder Charles Lochner wrote:

Winter in my life,
Ice upon my mind,
Thoughts that have no words,
Trust I cannot find.
How can I go on throughout the night?

Many years ago, Father Finn, I used to think of Job as being a patient man, but that was before I read the Book of Job and found out that he is one of the most impatient characters in the Bible. He doesn't talk to God, he screams:

I will give myself up to complaint;
I will speak from the bitterness of my soul.
I will say to God: Do not put me in the wrong!
Let me know why You oppose me.
Is it a pleasure for You to oppress,
to spurn the work of your hands? (Job 10:1-3)

And Moses was even more demanding when he prayed to God, "If this is the way you will deal with me, please do me the favor of killing me at once, so that I need no longer fear distress" (Numbers 11:14-15).

The late Jack Benny took a more whimsical attitude. Once, upon receiving an award he remarked, "I don't deserve this, but I have arthritis and I don't deserve that either."

In Prospect, Connecticut, in 1977, eight victims of the worst mass murder in the state's history, a young mother and her seven children, were buried side by side.

Thirty-four pall bearers carried the caskets to the Prospect Town Cemetery just across the road from the church—six pallbearers for 29-year-old Cheryl Beaudoin and four for each of her children.

"How could something like this happen?" Father Joseph Donnelly asked friends and relatives who crowded the 850-seat St. Anthony Padua Church to mourn the death of Mrs. Beaudoin and her children.

"Why does God let this go on? Why do the innocent suffer? And yet, as surely as we have all asked these questions, we have all found that there are no answers—none at all."

Christ, Himself, never gave us an answer as to the "why" of pain. All He did was to give us an example. "Not my will be done, but Thine."

In the *Christopher News Notes*, William J. Wilson tells us, "Ultimately there are no satisfactory answers to the question of pain and suffering. The hurt of life is not a problem to be solved. It is a process to be lived. Jesus shared our human life with all its grubbiness, exaltation and suffering."

In our aloneness and pain, there can be prayer. In her pain, Rosalind Russell prayed:

"Trust Him when darkest thoughts assail thee.
Trust Him when thy faith is small.
Trust Him when to simply trust Him
is the hardest thing of all."

Father John P. Daly, S.J., wrote, "When an accident strikes us or a loved one, when death calls, what is our first reaction? Sorrow, anger, disappointment? Then truly we need to say, 'I believe. I cannot understand why this happened to me or to my loved one, but I do believe, Lord.'"

St. Francis de Sales tells us: "Do not fear what may happen tomorrow. The same loving Father who cares for you today, will care for you tomorrow and everyday. Either He will shield you from suffering or He will give you unfailing strength to bear it. Be at peace, then, and put aside all anxious thoughts and imaginings."

There is nothing wrong with saying to God, "Lord, I'm really depressed today. I don't know how I can make it, but I'll try to put my trust in You. Help me." Many of the psalms express exactly the same sentiments!

I'm inspired, Father Finn, by the way you accepted the limitations put on your writing by circumstances beyond your control. Your sentiments are those expressed by John Milton in his poem "On His Blindness":*

When I consider how my light is spent
  Ere half my days, in this dark world and wide,
  And that one talent which is death to hide,
Lodged with me useless, though my soul
    more bent
  To serve therewith my Maker, and present
  My true account, lest He returning chide:
"Doth God exact day-labor, light denied?"
  I fondly ask: but Patience, to prevent

That murmur, soon replies, "God doth not need
  Either man's work or His own gifts: who best
  Bear His mild yoke, they serve Him best:
    His state
Is kingly; thousands at His bidding speed,
  And post o'er land and ocean without rest;
  They also serve who only stand and wait."

One of the most inspiring persons I've listened to on TV is Mr. Max Cleland, Administrator of the Veterans Administration, Washington, D.C.

In 1968, Captain Max Cleland was serving our country in Vietnam when a grenade exploded depriving him of both legs and an arm. Upon returning from Vietnam he spent 18 months in rehabilitation, then entered politics to become the youngest member of the Georgia State Senate, serving two terms from 1970-74. In 1975 he joined the U.S. Senate Veterans Affairs committee staff to work on health-care issues.

I was deeply moved when Max Cleland said the following prayer, which has become identified with him. He closes many of his speeches and interviews with it. The origin of the prayer is unknown, although it is believed to have been written by a Confederate soldier during the Civil War.

> I asked God for strength, that I might achieve,
> I was made weak, that I might learn humbly
>   to obey.
> I asked for health, that I might do greater things.
> I was given infirmity that I might do better things.
> I asked for riches, that I might be happy,
> I was given poverty, that I might be wise.
> I asked for power, that I might have the praise
>   of men,
> I was given weakness, that I might feel the need
>   of God.
> I asked for all things, that I might enjoy life,
> I was given life, that I might enjoy all things.
> I got nothing that I asked for—but everything
>   I had hoped for.
> Almost despite myself, my unspoken prayers
>   were answered.
> I am, among all men, most richly blessed.

The following thought of Cardinal Newman has helped many sick, lonely, and desperate people: "God beholds you individually whoever you are; He calls you by your name. He knows what is in you, all your own peculiar feelings and thoughts, your dispositions and likings, your strength and your weakness. He views you in the day of your rejoicing as well as in the day of your sorrow. He sympathizes in your hopes and your temptations. He interests Himself in all your anxieties and remembrances, all the risings and fallings of your soul. He has numbered all the hairs of your head. He compasses you round and bears you in His arms. He takes you up and puts you down. He notes your countenance, whether smiling or in tears. He looks tenderly upon your hands and feet. He hears your voice, the beating of your heart, and your very breathing. You do not love yourself better than He loves you. You cannot shrink from pain more than He dislikes you bearing it; and if He puts it on you, it is for a greater good."

No doubt, Father Finn, you read some of the poems of the poet-priest, Father John B. Tabb, who was fourteen years your senior. His poem, *Life's Weaving*, is a fitting climax to this chapter:**

My life is but a weaving
Between my God and me;
I may not choose the colors,
He knows what they should be;
For He can view the pattern
Upon the upper side
While I can see it only
On this, the under side.

Sometimes He weaveth sorrow
Which seemeth strange to me,
But I will trust His judgment
And work on faithfully.
'Tis He who fills the shuttle

He knows just what is best
So I shall weave in earnest
And leave with Him the rest.

At last, when life is ended
With Him I shall abide,
Then I may view the pattern
Upon the upper side
Then I shall know the reason
Why pain with joy entwined

Was woven in the fabric
Of life that God designed.

BERTA HUMMEL

The Happy Glow of Easter

Your name, Berta Hummel, evokes visions of winsome ceramics and charming greeting cards depicting children who walk familiarly with angels, or stand in sturdy reverence gazing up at silver stars in an evening sky.

One August, Berta, I was within a few miles of the Bavarian market town of Massing, not far from Munich, where you were born May 21, 1909.

As I traveled through this lovely countryside dotted with wayside shrines, I saw entire sides of houses painted with Gospel scenes, or illustrations from literature. Now I understand why in your life religion and art were one. Your memories were entwined with the eternal and the beautiful.

You were most fortunate, Berta, when you were in grade school, to have a nun teacher of deep understanding and exquisite sympathy who recognized your talents, and helped you to develop them.

At the age of twelve you entered the school in Simbach conducted by the "English Sisters" of the Institute of Mary. During these six years when you took up the study of art formally, your amazing progress indicated that the career of an artist would be yours.

In 1926, one year before Charles A. Lindbergh flew 3,610 miles from New York to Paris in his monoplane, *Spirit of St. Louis,* you entered the Art Academy of Munich. In 1931, you graduated at the age of 22 at the head of your class. Your skill and vision were such that your teachers predicted a brilliant future for you.

A month after your graduation from the Art Academy you entered the Franciscan Order and were given the name Sister Mary Innocentia.

The years following your religious profession in 1934 were sparkling with happiness. Your art work, under the name of Berta Hummel, was rapidly winning recognition. An enthusiastic friend published a *Hummel Book* of pictures. At the Leipzig fair in 1937 your figurines commanded rave notices from the critics.

Then came the cancer of madness that crept across Europe. Nazis despoiled your convent. The Sisters became prisoners in their own home. Extreme hardship and suffering took their toll. Your delicate health broke down completely. On November 6, 1946, at the age of thirty-seven you went forth into the joy of the Lord.

It is truly inspiring, Berta, to know that your ambition in life was to be an apostle of joy. You helped us all delight in the spiritual impact of simple things.

The twin stars around which your art orbited were the feasts of Christmas and Easter. Even when you were a young girl you found artistic expression of your faith at Easter time by decorating Easter eggs.

You would have been delighted, Berta, with the "Tree of Life" which Father Ed Thome had one Easter.

A small elm tree about four feet high was stuck in a pail of sand on the south side of the sacristy. When the children came to church on Holy Saturday and Easter Sunday, they were invited to bring Easter eggs to decorate the barren branches. (The eggs had a small hole punched in the large end of the shell, and a pin point hole at the smaller end. By blowing gently through the pin hole, the contents of the egg could be forced out the larger hole. The shells were then decorated. When they dried, a small loop of paper was pasted to the small end, so that the eggs could be suspended from a branch on the tree.)

On Holy Saturday I obtained one of the eggs that had not yet been painted, and took it with me into the pulpit on Easter Sunday. I began my sermon by holding up the egg for all to see, and then asking these questions, "Why do we have eggs at Easter? What is the symbol of the Easter egg?

"If you take an egg from the refrigerator," I continued, "it feels cold and lifeless as a tombstone. The hard, cold, white egg shell seems to hold no more life than a chunk of white marble.

"But look what would have happened if this egg had been left under a mother hen for three weeks. The egg would hatch. A baby chick would come out of the shell!

"Yet on first sight the egg seems cold and lifeless as a tombstone. The tombstone itself seems quite hopeless—on first sight. It seems to say, 'This is the end of everything.' Yet from that cold, barren-looking grave will come life. In the warmth and glory of your own personal resurrection, you will feel again the warm, pulsating spark of life. The words of Christ will ring true: 'I am the Resurrection and the Life; he who believes in me, even if he die, shall live.'"

The Easter egg is a symbol of the resurrection, a sign of life to come, a reminder that the cold grave will one day burst with life and light.

We do not know exactly when the egg was first associated with Easter, but the symbol of the chick breaking forth from the egg as the emergence of life from the sepulchre has persisted through long ages.

The decoration of eggs dates from thousands of years before Christianity. The egg is a natural symbol of life. By dyeing and adorning the egg the ancients transformed it into a thing of beauty to express their joy in the return of the warm sun with its life-giving force. Since these glorified eggs were exchanged among relatives and friends, the primitive designs of sunbursts or wheat or encircling lines symbolized the giver's heartfelt wishes for good health or bountiful harvests.

With the coming of Christianity, the decorated egg continued to be a symbol of life—but now with added victorious significance. The old triangular patterns, once standing for the three elements of air, fire and water, now stood for the Trinity of Father, Son, and Holy Spirit. The animals representing prosperity—the deer and the horses and rams—remained. But now they were joined by fish, the sign of mutual recognition among early Christians.

In no place in the world has the art of decorating the Easter egg been more beautifully perfected than in the Ukraine, now a republic of the Soviet Union. The beautifully decorated egg is called "pysanky."

Today in western Canada there are thousands of Ukrainians who still cherish their Easter traditions. Easter breakfast is served after an early-morning church service and Mass which includes the singing of the traditional Ukrainian hymn "Khrystos Voskres"— "Christ is Risen." The families return home, carrying with them blessed foods: "paska," an Easter bread which symbolizes the risen Lord; meat products, dairy products; and above all the pysanky (colored eggs).

The sharing of the Easter meal has a deep Biblical and liturgical meaning, and foreshadows our ultimate banquet with the Lord in heaven. Easter is called "Ve-lykden," the Great Day, and inspires special spring songs and choral dances.

The town of Vegreville, Alberta, has the most unique "pysanky" in the world. A 31-foot high egg is made of aluminum and decorated in intricate patterns of gold, black, and white.

One Sunday evening I attended an adult education class at Saint Gabriel's Parish. The visiting lecturer that evening was Father John Heagle. His message was most inspiring. "We know a secret that deserves to be shared, by allowing it to touch and strengthen our lives.

"Christianity does not have the answer for suffering. It is an invitation to enter into life. Christianity opens for us a window on a joyful eternity. Look where Christianity can take you—to the glory of your own resurrection!

"The most wonderful words of Christ are, 'I go to prepare a place for you, that where I am, you also may be, that your joy may be full.'

"The 'Good News' is that life is a gift that will blossom into resurrection. Christianity is a most enriching, mind-expanding way of life."

The theme of Father Heagle's talk was echoed and amplified a year later when I was in Nebraska, and heard a talk given by Father John Powell, S.J.

"Your destiny is heaven. God tells us, 'By all means join the dance and sing the songs of a full life. You are on your way to the happiness in heaven I have prepared for you. The sufferings of this present life are nothing compared to the glory and joy that will be yours.'

"Eye has not seen, nor ear heard, nor the mind of man ever imagined the joy I have prepared for you because you have opened yourself to my gift of love. On your way to heaven, enjoy the journey. Let your happiness be double, in the joyful possession of what you have and in the eager anticipation of what will one day be yours. Say a resounding 'Yes!' to life and to love at all times. Someday you will come up into my mountain, and then for you all the clocks and calendars will have finished their counting. Together with all my children, you will be mine, and I will be yours forever."

A friend of mine who was dying of cancer said, "Life on earth is only like a passing cloud or vapor. God and heaven are all. Without this conviction, both the torment of living, and the prospect of death would be unbearable."

There is no way to avoid suffering. It is up to us to give it eternal value by accepting it with equanimity of spirit for the love of God.

Because of Christ's resurrection we have been given a new birth, a birth unto hope, a birth to an imperishable inheritance which is kept in heaven for us. "There is cause here for rejoicing," says Saint Peter. "You may for a time, have to suffer the distress of many trials; but this is so that your faith, which is more precious than the passing splendor of fire-tried gold, may by its genuineness lead to praise, glory, and honor when Jesus Christ appears" (1 Peter 1:6-7).

Patience is hope in God's promises and confidence in His fatherhood. Many years ago Father Daniel A. Lord, S.J., said, "The lurid red of Good Friday is transmuted with a hardly perceptible break into the glorious pinks and scarlets of Easter's dawn. The broken body of God-made-man rises in a triumph of happiness that shall know no end. In the happiness of the risen Christ we read the happiness that in a measure will one day be our own.

"If the Church takes its members down into the forty days of Lent, it lifts them up to long months of happiness in the certain faith and convincing hope of a God triumphant over all suffering.

"Ours is a happy faith, my friends, and ahead of us now as throughout our life is the happy glow of Easter."

The rising of Christ gives to each of us an Easter of our own!

I have on my desk a beautiful booklet to commemorate the dedication of The Cathedral of the Risen Christ in Lincoln, Nebraska. The reason for this name being chosen for the cathedral is explained on page four of the inspiring booklet. "The resurrection of the first Easter is the central thought and mystery of Christianity. It is the heart of our faith and our hope. And so it is the theme of the new Cathedral. All things in the Cathedral of the Risen Christ tell of this truly tremendous event. The windows, the art work, the statuary announce as did the angel on Easter: 'He has risen even as He said. Alleluia!'"

"For me Easter means joy," says Juan Arias. "I know that Christ has risen, I feel it deep in my heart and it fills me with joy, joy because I feel that I am in communion with the Creator and with creation, joy at seeing myself reflected in the eyes of others, and at being able to say to them, 'We are new again!'"

The following message from Juan Arias vibrates like bugle notes with excitement and challenge: "Easter ought to be simply the day on which, in a very special way, we Christians cry out to each other, and especially the day when, all together, we cry out to the world the joy of our certainty of resurrection, the ecstasy of our new love, our hope of the final triumph of life over death."

Commenting on the mystery of life and death, Brother Tom Murphy, S.J., once remarked: "We are all terminal. The countdown began the day we were born. When the count goes down to zero, then, like a Saturn 5 rocket leaping towards the stars, we soar up into God's heavenly kingdom."

Alfred Lord Tennyson, the poet-laureate of England after Wordsworth's death, wrote, "Death is the bright side of life."

1979 was celebrated as the "Centennial of Light." It was on October 21, 1879, that Thomas Alva Edison invented the first practical incandescent light bulb in Menlo Park, New Jersey.

Among the many interesting anecdotes that appeared in newspapers and magazines · was one reported to have been told by Mrs. Edison concerning the death of her famous husband. Mrs. Edison and the doctor were standing by the bed of Thomas when it became evident that he was at death's door, and wanted to say something to them. They bent down closely over the scientific genius. With a smile on his face Thomas Edison murmured, "It is very beautiful over there."

In a beautiful, inspiring letter he wrote to Saint Bonaventure, Pope John Paul I said that in resurrecting Christ, God the Father glorified His humanity and the humanity of all those who are His, "joyously announcing that the whole world will one day be transformed into a 'new heaven and a new earth.'"

Peter A. Leischner, an eighteen-year-old senior at St. John Vianney Seminary, Richmond, Virginia, knew for a year and a half that he was dying of leukemia. But Peter faced death without any fear and anticipated it joyfully. He wanted his funeral to be joyful and planned many details of his Mass the night before he died, January 22, 1976. The attitude of Peter A. Leischner is similar to that of the Polish saint, Stanislaus Kostka. When informed that he was about to die, he replied in the words of the psalmist, "I rejoice at the things that are told unto me. We shall go into the house of the Lord."

Some five hundred years before the coming of Christ, the Greek poet Pindar wrote, "We are things of a day. The shadow of a dream is man, no more. But when the brightness comes, and God gives it, there is a shining of light on men, and their life is sweet."

Your heroic endurance, Berta, during your final years of suffering remind us that the joy of the Spirit, which should be the hallmark of a Christian, is not an emotional thing. It is an intellectual conviction that—despite all the pain and suffering—life is worthwhile, because it leads to joy and happiness in heaven above.

Over a quarter of a century ago Father Vincent McCorry, S.J., remarked, "There are peaks of satisfaction in every human life, and it is usually in connection with these high moments of existence that we use the strong word 'happiness.' We speak of the happiness of a bride, or of a proud mother, or the winner of a scholarship. But these strong joys are likewise rare joys.

"It is not really pertinent to ask an ordinary person on an ordinary day whether or not he or she is happy. Yet on an ordinary day an ordinary person ought to be ordinarily content. They need not regularly shout for joy or habitually throw their hats in the air; but they should be at least normally contented. A person should be 'happy in his vocation,' not enthusiastic perhaps, but fundamentally satisfied. Obviously, fundamental satisfaction may coexist with accidental dissatisfaction."

The heroism of most of us will spring from the commonplace material of everyday existence. The majority of us have no dramatic Good Friday; just a monotonous grindstone of exasperating details that chip our patience like a carborondum wheel.

Too many people seem to have lives that are bleak as the moon. Nothing of consequence happens to them. Perhaps the biggest thing in their week is the next episode of their favorite TV show, or a copy of a national newspaper that someone left on a crosstown bus. When we try to discover just what we actually accomplish on some days, the answer is, "Not very much." We find that almost all jobs have their quota of routine tasks that are repetitive and dull.

Life is something like Swiss cheese—full of empty spaces. We spend much time just waiting, and wishing for things to happen.

The great, outstanding mountain peaks in our lives are so distant and far-spaced, that we look forward to them, and backward to them from the level plain of our existence.

It has been said that the greatest benefit from a vacation is not merely the few days we spend in the mountains, or on the seashore, but rather, the mental lift we experience during the long weeks of planning, and then, the joy we experience when we recall the vacation in memory, and re-live it via snapshots and 8mm movies.

Some days we may feel as though we are strolling on Cloud Number Nine. We hold the world in our embrace. We are intoxicated with memories that have been sweetened through the ages, just like wine.

Then come the cloud-filled nights when the rocket of hope that once leaped to the sky cascading golden sparks of hope, falls to earth, a dead stick. Even the stars desert the sky.

We open our mouths to pray, but the words we wanted to say vanish in a swallow down our throats.

The story is told of a man who had been planning to take a bio-feedback course, but then, he gave up the idea. He figured he had enough bad news already.

The chemistry of internal feelings amazes and startles, and, at times, even frightens us. Some days we feel like a sugar cube filled to the edges with sweetness. Other days we feel like an old shingle on the north side of a barn.

In a special series of adult education classes held in Prairie du Chien, Wisconsin, Dr. Eugene Kinder of the Crawford County Counseling Center stated that "It's normal to feel depressive 'gloom clouds' hanging over our shoulders now and then. You can't avoid depression. Its origins are not something you have control over. You might be feeling depressed and then one day you notice you are not depressed any more. It's like a dream—it just went away.

"Being depressed," continued Dr. Kinder, "is a part of being a human being. Everyone has some contact with depression in their lives regardless of age."

Some are torn more than others by the contradictions of their moods. The biography of Audubon comments that he "always pursued a zigzag course between high elation and dark spirits." Goethe remarked that Beethoven was either "exulting to heaven" or "dejected to death."

We all are in danger of moody reactions under the tensions of a hard day, and when circumstances seem to go against us. Worry can gnaw away at the edges of a person's mind until it feels as though spiders were crawling around inside the skull.

And the more one thinks of all the evil things that may happen, the worse the situation becomes, until one feels as though he is sitting on a keg of TNT about to explode.

In our moments of discouragement it is worth remembering Christ on His cross. At that point, His message and His work seemed to have come to an inglorious end. His love for all men and women seemed wasted. His message of the brotherhood under God appeared to be totally wounded by the spear that pierced His side.

But the Easter that came after the Good Friday made everything different from what had gone before. The saga of Christ's death and resurrection is an antidote for discouragement. It gives us courage to press on in the service of the good.

Each of us has to be at peace, feeling a certain amount of confidence toward what we are and what we can't change and a sense of how to reach to things we can change.

There is no meaning in life unless there is a certain amount of reason to it. Having values enables you to put meaning or derive meaning from your life and your efforts. There is satisfaction in knowing that we have a philosophy of life based on the words of Christ, "Be glad and rejoice because your reward is great in heaven."

Hubert H. Humphrey, the dynamic senator from Minnesota, who died from cancer admitted that "most of us have enough problems so that almost any day we could fold up and say, 'I've had it.'"

At one time when he was taking X-Ray treatments, Humphrey was tormented in the night by bladder spasms. "I was in such agony," he said, "that I honestly wanted to give it all up."

Humphrey went on to say that even in the deepest despair we have to keep our eyes on the mountaintop. Our life is not entirely in our own hands. There is a power beyond our own—God.

One afternoon in the hospital was especially depressing for Hubert. His wife, Muriel, told him that the previous evening she was so angry with God she cried, and kept asking, "Why you?"

In reply Hubert admitted that he, too, was puzzled. He did not know why he had to suffer so.

With utter honesty Hubert admitted, "Like anybody else's, my faith is sometimes rocked. When I'm feeling low, I draw strength from the prayer of St. Francis of Assisi."

This beautiful prayer reads:

Lord, make me an instrument of Your peace.
Where there is hatred, let me sow love.
Where there is injury, pardon.
Where there is doubt, faith.
Where there is despair, hope.
Where there is darkness, light.
Where there is sadness, joy.
O Divine Master, grant that I may not
    so much seek
To be consoled, as to console,
To be understood, as to understand;
To be loved, as to love, for
It is in giving, that we receive.
It is in pardoning, that we are pardoned,
It is in dying, that we are born to eternal life.

The prayer of St. Francis of Assisi made headlines when Margaret Hilda Thatcher, at the age of 53, became the first woman Prime Minister of Britain. When

Margaret Thatcher arrived at No. 10 Downing Street, the official residence of Prime Ministers, the street was packed with well-wishers and photographers.

Expressing delight and excitement over her victory, Britain's "Iron Lady" made a conciliatory statement clearly addressed to a nation poised uneasily for change: "I would like to remember some words of St. Francis of Assisi, which I think are particularly apt at the moment: 'Where there is discord, may we bring harmony; where there is doubt, may we bring faith; where there is despair, may we bring hope.' Now that the election is over, may we get together and strive to serve and strengthen the country."

JOHN PAUL I

The Face Value of a Smile

You, Pope John Paul I, deserve mention in the *Guinness Book of World Records*. In just thirty-four short days you conquered the world with a smile!

In the short time that elapsed between your election on August 26, 1978, and your death on September 28, 1978, you left no record of encyclicals, or papal policy, or great innovation. You scored your victory by a record of little and loving things. You became a harbinger of hope. Your style vibrated across the airwaves and delighted our sensitivities.

No wonder that on the day of your funeral Carlo Cardinal Confalonieri said that you were "a meteor that unexpectedly lights up the heavens and then disappears, leaving us amazed and astonished." One month was enough for you to win our hearts. It is not the length which characterizes the life of a pontificate, but rather the spirit that fills it.

Archbishop Daniel Sheehan of Omaha, in opening his homily at a memorial Mass for you, said: "We were all delighted when we saw him, and he immediately became the favorite of the entire world. Our encounter with him was a brief one, but we are certainly better for it. There was something about the happy, smiling presence of Pope John Paul I that thrilled everyone.

"We are confident," continued Archbishop Shee-han, "that this happy smile (of John Paul I) is now charming and delighting the angels and saints in heaven."

By your words and actions, Pope John Paul I, you offered an example of Christian joy and hope. You encouraged us to believe and live with openness, faith and service to the needs of others. You challenged us to be entirely human, fully alive.

The first American layman to be received in private audience by you, Pope John Paul I, was Supreme Knight of Columbus, Virgil C. Dechant. Concerning his private audience, he said that you came through as a "very warm, human and humble" person. You were very attentive to visitors, and punctuated your conversation with an ever ready smile.

When Virgil Dechant learned of your death, he wrote: "Rarely has a spiritual leader so little known captured the hearts of so many in so short a span of time. His most endearing qualities were his meekness and his compassionate heart open to every human and humane aspiration. It was this loving heart, pouring out solicitous concern for all mankind, that won our love in return."

Father Robert Kraus, S.J., editor of *The Jesuit Bulletin*, wrote concerning you, Pope John Paul I, "With his broad and sincere smile, his humility and simplicity, his pastoral approach with the ability to teach the truths of religion clearly, vitally and interestingly, the choice of John Paul I was a popular one."

You will be remembered, Pope John Paul I, for your human qualities rather than for your official actions. You will be remembered for your smile, your warmth, your delight in laughter and natural human contact—evidenced, as one observer put it, by your "almost compulsive need to hug everyone" you met.

It was during the Wednesday audiences, which were always filled to capacity, that your humanity and humor became the most apparent. On your way to the throne, you could not resist making human contact as you made your way through the crowds, shaking hands and kissing babies.

The reactions around the world that followed the news of your death, Pope John Paul I, were interesting. "So soon?" cried Manila's stunned Jaime Cardinal Sin. Said Cologne's Joseph Hoffner: "God has willed it as painful as His will is." And Paris' François Cardinal Marty: "The ways of the Lord are disconcerting to our human perspective." The late Humberto Cardinal Medeiros admitted, "I've been trying to say to God, 'It's your doing, and I must accept it.'"

The Netherlands' Johannes Cardinal Willebrands said, "his death reminds us how small and how weak man is, that life and death are mysteries, that we are in God's hands. That is why we also have faith."

Dale Francis said, "When you believe in heaven, you can't really have sorrow at the death of a good man. Pope John Paul I smiled, and there was no affectation. The world responded to the goodness of this man. He was a good man who obviously loved people. He just showed goodness and love, he was simply a man obviously of God, and no one doubted it. He brought great happiness into the world, and with it hope."

The influence of your life, Pope John Paul I, reminds me of the following words from the pen of an unknown poet:

Drop a pebble in the water,
And its ripples reach out far;
And the sunbeams dancing on them
May reflect them to a star.

Give a smile to someone passing,
Thereby making his morning glad;
It may greet you in the evening
When your own heart may be sad.

Do a deed of simple kindness;
Though its end you may not see,
It may reach, like widening ripples,
Down a long eternity.

By the example of your life, Pope John Paul I, you gave proof to the words of Dr. Norman Vincent Peale, "We create around us, always, an aura or an atmosphere or a climate by the kind of thoughts we think. And people pick up that climate and respond to us accordingly."

No wonder that William L. Stidger said, "We all become like that with which we live, like that which we look upon, read, or hear. If we like beautiful things, we become beautiful in our spirit. Those who see to it that only beautiful thoughts are accepted as guests in their homes and hearts become beautiful through constant contact with high and holy thinking."

Out of our eyes will look the spirit we have chosen. In our smile or frown the years will speak. As year adds to year the face will take lines to itself, like the parchment of an old historian who jealously sets down all the story.

There, deeper than acids etch steel, will be marked the narrative of our mental habits, the emotions of our heart, our sense of conscience, our response to duty, what we think of God, our fellow men, and ourself. It will all be there, for we become like that which we love, and the same thereof is written on our brows. We shall gather to ourselves the images we love.

Life's evening will take its character from the day that preceded it. We are shaped and fashioned by what we love. Just as the food we eat becomes part of our body, the nourishment that we give our mind becomes part of our way of thinking, although we are not always conscious of this "mental digestion."

Kirby Page informs us that we do not live by bread alone, but by the sweet song of a mockingbird, the magic of the maestro's violin, the grandeur of Handel's *Messiah*, the sublimity of Beethoven's *Fifth Symphony*.

Noted in literature for millennia is the concept that appearance mirrors the soul. Socrates admitted that once his face was stupid and sensual, before he improved it by studying philosophy.

Shakespeare frequently referred to connections between psyche and outward appearance, as in Viola's remark to the handsome captain in *Twelfth Night:* "There is a fair behavior in thee, captain...I will believe thou hast a mind that suits with this thy fair and outward character."

In his essay on beauty, Ralph Waldo Emerson expressed his firm belief that the cultivation of inner beauty manifests itself in outer comeliness. He also noted that eloquence or a fascinating personality transforms an ugly person into an attractive one.

A similar view was expressed at the turn of the century by New York physician Charles H. Shepard advising women on health and beauty: "Cultivate noble thoughts, for they serve to mold the countenance. The highest beauty is that of expression."

Dr. W. R. C. Latson added, "No woman is to blame if she is not beautiful at fifteen; but any woman is to blame if she is not beautiful before she reaches forty. The habitual mental state is the most powerful influence in promoting or destroying beauty. To think well is to look well. Beauty is everything but skin deep; it involves the entire personality of the individual."

There is a saying that goes something like this: "At twenty, you have the face you inherited; at forty, the face you developed; at sixty, the face you deserve." All the good deeds and good times are written there.

Naomi Sims of New York City, a writer, businesswoman, and one of America's most original and successful wig designers says, "I feel that true beauty must be a reflection of the spirit."

Sylvia Blythe wrote a fascinating article years ago with the title, "Your Face Is a Transparent Mask." A face is always a mirror of past emotions and experiences. Habits of serenity, of seeing things in perspective, of generosity and self-forgetfulness create a lovely image.

"This is quite literally true," says Sylvia. "The muscles of your face make an automatic external response to the emotions and moods that go on within.

Fewer facial muscles are called into play in response to happy thoughts. And the lines which such thoughts trace are pleasant.

"Anger, discontent, habitual peevishness, moods of petty envy and resentment, on the other hand, make your face pay the price.

"One of the best beauty treatments in the world," says Sylvia, "is to spend time with or let your thoughts dwell on someone who really loves you. You see this beauty in a woman who is happily in love—for there is no masking the brightness of her inner life."

Now and then we see adult faces that look as though a warm light were reflected through them from deep within. Such faces are beautiful. Often it is the eyes that produce this effect of inner radiance. Beauty of this kind is wholly independent of the contours of a face, or the shape of the features. These, when you analyze them, may prove to be commonplace. But the chances are that you will not feel an impulse to analyze.

Ginger Rogers is known for the stunning musical productions she innovated with Fred Astaire, and for the fashions she helped to establish.

A reporter asked Ginger, "What's the first thing you notice about a person?"

In reply, Ginger said, "Attitude. For me, the only true beauty is the quality of one's thought. If you harbor callous, negative, disorganized, petulant, angry thoughts, you are going to project that image—and attract those same ugly reactions.

"I believe that beauty is a quality with which we are all endowed—a gift from our Creator. But it's up to us to get it all out. That's why I think it's terribly important for all of us to use our best qualities to their advantage."

It is interesting, Pope John Paul I, to read what you said concerning the beauty of women in your letter to Maria Teresa of Austria, "Parents, brothers, and above all husbands want their women to be beautiful and elegant, but within a frame of modesty which makes them even more beautiful and morally fresh."

It is interesting to note that—according to the findings of psychologists—beauty and attractiveness are definitely not the same and that "even a high degree of beauty may have a low degree of attractiveness." A strikingly beautiful woman may have a cool, aloof or self-centered manner that minimizes her attractiveness. Conversely, a plainer woman's pleasing personality may do more to make her attractive to the opposite sex than the facial features of a classic beauty.

Surface features often play a smaller part in attraction than many people suppose, and romantic love, "especially when it leads to marriage, tends to stress much more vital traits of character and temperament."

Famed designer of high fashions, Emilio Pucci says, "When woman is reduced to a statue, that is all she is. In my opinion a woman's greatest qualities are her feminity, gracefulness, and mystery."

Rene Bouche, one of the most sought-after portraitists of American and international society, says that "elegance is probably the most appealing quality a man finds in a woman. Elegance comes from within a person's character and consequently does not depend on class or money. It's found among all social-economic groups. It is even independent of age."

No wonder it is said that our lives are what our thoughts make them. Wherever your heart is, whatever your thoughts are, you will be just that.

Every man's work is always a living portrait of himself!

"It does not take long," said Dwight L. Moody, "to tell where a man's treasure is. In fifteen minutes' conversation with most men you can tell whether their treasures are on the earth or in heaven."

In this chapter, Pope John Paul I, I made reference to the fact that the face is the mirror of the soul. Imagine my delight when I found this fact illustrated in *The Catholic Voice*, the archdiocesan newspaper, of Omaha, Nebraska.

The article relates how the editors of the *Interchurch Features*, an informal association of nine U.S. and Canadian church publications, worked for more than a year to choose six women as "Living Christian heroines worthy of recognition." "Their words and actions have transformed the lives of thousands of people; their lives exemplify what it means to be Christian." These six women are:

Mother Teresa, the Albanian nun who established the Missionaries of Charity in 1948 to serve the sick, the destitute and abandoned of the world, and whose Order now has more than 1,300 members working in 67 countries.

Dorothy Day, who co-founded the Catholic Worker Movement with the credo of "immediate response to the need of the other person."

Barbara Ward, a British writer, lecturer and philosopher who Ms. Purden said has become "the Christian conscience reminding us that we are our brother's and sister's keeper."

Corrie Ten Boom, who was imprisoned by the Nazis during World War II for aiding Jews in Holland and has spent the years since then lecturing and writing about the message of forgiveness and hope she learned in the Nazi concentration camp.

Lee Tai-Young, the first woman lawyer in South Korea and founder of the Korean Legal Aid Center for Family Relations.

Annie Jiagge, the first woman admitted to the bar in Togo, Africa, a leader in world ecumenism and "a champion for the rights of women" on an international basis.

The composite picture of the six women illustrated dynamically the very thing mentioned in this chapter. The beauty of each woman's character shines forth in her face, and, above all, in her eyes.

A number of years ago a distinguished Christian scholar, J. B. Phillips, drew up a list of what he considered to be the hallmarks of a Christian. They are:

Tranquillity of mind.
Unquenchable joy of spirit.
Outgoing love.

To these three hallmarks, Dr. Norman Vincent Peale added a fourth:

An irrepressible sense of victory.

These four hallmarks, Pope John Paul I, are all found in your life. The example of your life proclaims the "Good News" of the Gospel, which tells us that as children of God we can never say that we are defeated. We can handle any difficulty. We can stand up to any tragedy or sorrow, no matter how great it is. We can reach our goal regardless of the opposition and the setbacks that may face us. We can overcome anything, even death.

True, we may meet with temporary defeat. We may be torn with anguish. Wires of pain may pull our nerves. Loneliness may parch our heart. Our eyes may smart with tears, but the temporary affliction we all go through in this life is but a preparation for a lasting life of joy and happiness beyond all compare.

This wonderful new life is waiting for us, even now. Each day brings us 24 hours closer to the great day of final victory and unbounded joy.

No wonder St. Paul exhorts us to remember that death is not the end of life, but the beginning of life. "The present burden of our trial is light enough, and earns for us an eternal weight of glory beyond all comparison" (1 Cor. 4:17).

Perhaps the one thing for which you are remembered most of all, Pope John Paul I, is your smile. A smile reflects a certain permanent attitude toward life, toward others. A smile shows that deep in the heart there is a constant attitude of sympathy; the wish to share, not to dominate, to live in union with others; the desire to spread, not antagonism, but joy and love.

A smile is the key that unlocks the door to beauty and loveliness. A smile is an outer reflection of an inner condition. When such emotions are deeply felt, the thought shines through the countenance.

The story is told of a little girl on a summer morning standing in a great cathedral. The sunlight streamed through the beautiful stained-glass windows, and the figures in them of the servants of God were bright with brilliant color. A little later the question was asked, "What is a saint?" The girl replied, "A saint is a person who lets the light shine through them."

You, Pope John Paul I, are such a person. The light shines in your smile.

No wonder that Archbishop Sheehan said, "We are confident that this happy smile is now charming and delighting the angels and saints in heaven."

MY MOTHER

You Made Friends by Being One

The term "Golden Age" is sometimes used to refer to the fact that a person is past 65 years of age. The term is also used as an expression of spirit and mind. Taken in this meaning, the Golden Age is timeless. It is always in the human heart, sometimes quietly, sometimes exultantly.

The people who live a Golden Age may be six years old, or sixteen, or sixty. These people break through the boundaries of time. Changing days and years do not constrain them. But the ticking of the second hand drives them on. Their world is limitless, new, and exciting. Theirs is the expanding universe.

These are the people who are never too tired to seek. They are impelled to activity, either of mind or body, or both.

You, Mother, belong to this Golden Age. You were one of those inspiring persons who was fully "involved in life." Your home was like a lighthouse flashing a beacon of happiness and joy to all around. Neighbors loved to stop in to visit you.

By the example of your life, you proved the words of A. Nielen, "Happiness adds and multiplies as we divide it with others."

You loved people. Your love went out to everyone. You shared their lives, their joys, their misfortunes. You were continually collecting used items of clothing and household articles for the needy. You visited the sick, and lavished your time and devotion on them.

Despite work-filled days, you found time to write many beautiful and inspiring articles, which appeared in national magazines over a period of many years.

When Mrs. T. Flynt of Phoenix, Arizona, heard of your death, she wrote to me, "Your mother had such a marvelous mind, and was so articulate. She was a person who gave so much happiness to so many. She had such an interest in people."

My sister, Mrs. Rex Gobel wrote of you, "What a legacy to leave to others. Her consuming love of people and life animated that spirit in a manner seldom seen. Despair and defeat simply weren't in her reckoning."

By the example of your life, Mother, you proved that a very important thing in a person's life is his or her mental attitude. Each life at the moment is but the massed results of the mental attitude of the yesterdays.

All that a person does outwardly is but the expression and completion of his or her inward thought. To work effectively, a person must think clearly; to act nobly, a person must think nobly.

One of the loveliest tributes paid to you, Mother, was that penned by your close neighbor and life-long friend, Mrs. Ceil Fitzpatrick: "I loved to see her flowers, and more than their beauty, I believe her joy was in being a part of their growing.

"Just after she came home from the hospital this past summer, when I went to see her, she walked right to the back door to show me a yellow lily.

"The predominant thought in my mind will always be her witty little remark, followed by a soft smile, which usually developed into a hearty laugh. I repeat, she was an extraordinary person, and we'll miss her."

You had for your natural endowment, Mother, that which is undoubtedly one of the greatest natural personal gifts—enthusiasm. Everything in the world you found exciting. Everyone you met stimulated and aroused your interest. The past you found romantic; the present you found unendingly delightful; the future you saw through the purple haze of optimistic hope.

You loved to hold high converse with friends at home, or with chance acquaintances riding with you on a train or bus. When you gave book reviews in Omaha, Nebraska, you found so much delight in the subject you were handling that your infectious joy went right down into the hearts of your listeners.

You were always looking for the surprise and delight that lies in everything and everybody. Even such prosaic tasks as washing clothes, ironing, and preparing meals you approached like an artist creating a masterpiece.

You found the whole world a place of magic and mystery and surprises and delights, of glorious revelations of man's wonderful nature, of astounding glimpses of the glory of the world's Creator.

You lived with eyes open wide to the wonders about you, and with ears attuned to the earth's endless melodies.

Time and again our neighbors on Webster Street remarked to me how on a bright summer morning they delighted to listen to you singing as you went about the task of hanging the clothes on the clothesline to dry.

As you moved from enthusiasm to enthusiasm, your life grew richer, your experience more varied, your knowledge constantly deeper and clearer, your human sympathies more enveloping, your own soul a thing of endless lights.

Someone has stated: "Beautiful young people are a creation of nature. Beautiful old people create themselves." You, Mother, created a wealth in your thoughts and emotions. You lived in the eternal now by seeking to get the most out of each precious moment by having an open heart, and an open mind. You shared your love and happiness with others. Your positive, constructive attitude made your spirit so radiant, no one ever noticed the wrinkles. Your beauty came from your mind, not from a jar of face cream. Your calendar showed the passing of time—your face showed what you were doing with it.

By the example of your life, Mother, you proved that those people are a success who have laughed often, and loved much; who gained the respect of the intelligent, and the love of children; who never lacked appreciation of earth's beauty nor failed to express it; who looked at the best in others, and gave the best they had.

Mrs. T. Flynt once sent you a greeting card with the following poem by Eleanor Long:

A friend is someone lovely, who
Cuts her chrysanthemums for you

And, giving, cares not for the cost,
Nor sees the blossoms she has lost;
But rather, values friendship's store
Gives you her best and grows some more.

Underneath this poem Mrs. Flynt had written this note to you, Mother: "The above is a true description of you, my dear."

You brought drama and poetry into the lives of your children, Mother, and transformed what seemed a prosaic task of daily existence into an epic saga, into a quest for the Holy Grail.

You, Mother, introduced us children to music via the most beautiful instrument in the world—the human voice. Nature had gifted you with a beautiful voice, and song rose to your lips as naturally as the morning sun rose over the high mountains of the Continental Divide just east of Butte, Montana.

Our modest, little home echoed to the beautiful melodies of "The Rosary," "When Irish Eyes are Smiling," "Let Me Call You Sweetheart," "Meet Me Tonight in Dreamland," and "Mother Machree."

Down the arches of the years those words from "Mother Machree" echo with a poignancy that increases with time: "There's a place in my memory, my life that you fill, no other can take it, no one ever will."

I once had the good fortune of visiting Australia. While there, I descended into the famed Jenolan Caves some ninety miles to the west of Sydney. After following the guide for over half an hour through the labyrinthian maze of tunnels, we climbed a steep incline that led into the "Cathedral Room."

The guide threw an electric switch, and the cathedral-like cave became alive with myriad lights artistically placed at the most dramatic spots to bring out the glittering beauty of this underground masterpiece of nature.

The dazzling beauty of the room was overwhelming. Tremendous stalactites soared in gleaming arcs over my head as though they never heard of the law of gravity. Ceiling and walls looked as though they had been dipped in rainbows. Along the walls, drops of water jumped softly on little bare feet to dance in pools in the hearts of stalagmites.

The guide turned on a second switch that activated a tape recorder and the "Cathedral" was flooded with the incomparable voice of John McCormick singing "The Rosary."

"How strange," I thought, "to be hearing my mother's beloved on the other side of planet earth, and deep within the earth in the 'Land Down Under.'"

With the coming of late May to the Montana mountains, Mother, you marshaled the help of us children in transforming our yard into a beauty spot. Along the trellis-like fence on the west side of our back yard, we planted sweet peas. In the front yard, in the little space between the porch and walk, we planted nasturtiums and pansies. When these delightful pansies bloomed they reminded me of little elves that peered above a leaf to blink with tiny and delightful faces.

The rocky soil, cool nights, and the short growing season in our mile-high city of Butte, in the heart of the Rocky Mountains, limited the choice of flowers for the garden.

When we came to Omaha, the climate and soil made many more flowers possible. Our yard became a carnival of colors.

In April, when spring came leaping over the garden fence, you delighted in the color-splashed tulips. With heads erect, as straight and tall as if by some proud monarch sent, the tulips marched along your garden wall, a gold and crimson regiment, the first troopers to invade the yard after the long siege of winter.

Catching the tempo of spring, sturdy iris leaped like flags of glory to the sky, unfurling rainbow colors along the east side of the house.

With the coming of May the lilacs in the backyard swayed in lavender mist and intoxicated the spring zephyr with perfume all pervading and perfuse.

Next came eager peonies reaching for the sky, and bursting into snowballs of dazzling white. Along the alley a triple row of hollyhocks began to build a fence of their own around our yard.

Among all the floral wonders in your garden, Mother, the flowers that held the Number One position in your heart were the roses. You loved the floribunda roses with summer-long blooms in bouquet clusters; the hybrid tea roses with blooms large and usually fragrant, often on single stems, splendid for cutting as well as for garden display. Your climbing roses by the side of the garage were so eager, they climbed over everything in sight.

To you, Mother, I adapt the words of a poet:

"All kindly things were sister to your soul;
Evil you scorned, and hated every wrong;
Gentle, another's wounds oft wounded you."

"The person who makes room in his heart for others, will find accommodations everywhere." These words of an unknown author are true of you, Mother.

Much as you enjoyed life, you looked forward with even greater interest to our life to come. Time and again when you received word that someone you knew, who had been suffering for a long time, had died, your reply always was: "Thank God! Their suffering is over. Now they can enjoy the happiness God made for them."

You informed us children that after your death, we were not to cry. As soon as the funeral was over, we were to come together for a family picnic.

On September 20, 1969, I was at Campion High School. Since Campion was a boarding school, we had class until noon on Saturday. It was early morning. I was in my room preparing for class work for that day when I received a long distance phone call from my sister, Mary, in Omaha, Nebraska, informing me that you, Mother, had died early that morning at Bergan Mercy Hospital.

Immediately after the phone call I said, "Thank You, God, for taking Mother from the pain and suffering of planet earth into the glory and joy of Your heavenly home."

My next prayer was to congratulate you, Mother, on your "birthday." (In the early ages of the Church, the day on which a person died was considered to be his or her true "birthday"—and so it is—his or her "birthday" into joy and happiness unbounded.)

That afternoon as I rode the bus from Prairie du Chien to Omaha, I looked up at the beautiful blue September sky, and thought of the sentiments expressed by Michael Kent on the first page of his book, *The Mass of Brother Michael*: "It was a perfect day on which to die, if one believed death to be a birth, and a beginning, a reward, and a release. The air was a crystal transparency, charged with a magic that sharpened the edges and heightened the colors of all things. The cloudless sky was no mere emptiness, but an inverted sea, a swimming blue depth and intensity, in which the birds, plunging upward, were lost in flight."

Recently, when I picked up a copy of *The Catholic Voice* for the Archdiocese of Omaha, I was delighted to find that the death notices were listed under a glorious masthead, which read:

"RESURRECTION JOY THIS WEEK FOR:"

(There followed the names of those who had entered into eternity during the past seven days.)

MY DAD

Duty, Honor, Devotion!

Like a delicate cloud of bugle notes, three words vibrate in the crisp, morning air. These words stand for the ideals by which you, Dad, guided your life, much as mariners of old guided their ships by the light from distant stars. They are: duty, honor, devotion!

The stern virtue of duty most likely would not win a popularity contest in today's pleasure-seeking society, hence it is doubly inspiring to know a man who guided his life by this lofty star.

The question you always asked yourself first and foremost was, "What should I do?" Personal satisfaction and questions of ease and convenience never entered the picture. And once you made a decision, you stuck by it, no matter what the cost.

You never drank, smoked, gambled, or belonged to any clubs. You never played golf and never had a car. You took the streetcar or bus to work, or walked, if possible.

You did not spend money on yourself. Were it not for the family, you would never have had new clothes to wear. Like so many people who existed through the Great Depression, you were most careful with every dollar. You thoroughly disliked the idea of buying things on credit. Your motto was, "Pay cash, or don't bother."

Honor was more than a word for you, Dad; it was your way of life. By your life you gave proof to Shakespeare's words: "This, above all, to thine own self be true, and it must follow as the night the day, thou cans't not then be false to any man."

Your word was your honor. You were honest as the day was long. You took things at face value, and you held in utter contempt anyone who used philosophical distinctions to whittle away truth to the vanishing point.

According to Harold Blake Walker, loyalty to the ultimate values of life in a moment of testing is evidence of the current of a life. Behind the hour of courageous decision are gathered the decisions and choices of the years that fling themselves like a torrent against the issue of the hour. People who keep their integrity intact do so because they are sustained by the flowing torrent of their choices made yesterday and the days before.

People who worked with you, Dad, often remarked that you were one hundred percent trustworthy. When you made a promise, you stood by it, no matter what the inconvenience to yourself. You were always on time, hard-working, and thoroughly dependable.

Your life was exact and orderly as an engineer's blueprint. Even at the age of seventy you were setting footings for the Manelli Construction Company. You took pride in the fact that none of the buildings for which you set the footings ever cracked or settled.

Your training in engineering at the Armour Institute in Chicago enabled you to estimate the stresses that various materials could carry.

Carved in stone on one of the state buildings in Sacramento, California, are these words: "Bring me men to match my mountains."

You, Dad, were truly a man "to match the mountains"—both in your rugged physique and stalwart moral qualities. Some of our neighbors remarked that you must truly be "the last of the mountain men."

Some of our neighbors thought of you as "the John Wayne of Webster Street." Your words were few and to the point. You shied away from showing affection in public. You were independent, and self-sufficient, as became a man who had spent so many years in the far West.

Your introduction to the West began in March, 1908, when you went to Council Bluffs, Iowa, and climbed into an emigrant car (a box car) with your dad and prepared to ship to Campstool, Wyoming, to take up a homestead. With you in the box car were a team of horses, a cow, a crate of chickens, a wagon, a dog, and some farm and household articles. It took the Union Pacific freight train eight days to Campstool, some 15 miles east of Cheyenne.

At Campstool the emigrant car was set on a side track, and unloaded. You hauled your belongings by horse and wagon to the land you were to homestead, and dumped them on the spot. The next day you ran lines to determine the central point of the section. (A section of land is 1 mile square, or 640 acres.) After locating the center of the section you got some lumber and put up a shack.

Alas, the irrigation project that had been promised to the homesteaders did not come true. Left to itself the land produced only tumbleweeds and cactus and sage, and so, in 1910, you went to Twin Falls, Idaho.

Religion to you, Dad, was not something to be put on like a tie or vest on Sunday morning when you go to church. Religion for you was part of your very life-blood and fiber.

Time and again neighbors remarked how they would see you in St. Cecilia's Cathedral saying your Rosary. "When you look at Mr. Scott when he is saying his prayers," the neighbors said, "you know that you are looking at a man who sees God."

According to social scientists, "the parents' religious behavior is more important than the parish, school, and Church pronouncements in determining whether or not a child will become a lifelong church-going Catholic."

Dr. James Herzog of the Harvard Medical School says that the mother is the one who nurtures the child's sense of self, who provides warmth and a sense of being loved and cherished.

The father, on the other hand, does all this, but he also provides the child a role of a person who can, in a sense, stand back from life and view it with a sense of perspective.

This I know for sure. Your example, Dad, and that of Mother, made God comfortable in the family, and the family comfortable with God.

I came across a statement by Clare Boothe Luce that made me think of you, Dad: "Today there is a lot of talk about fulfilling yourself and seeking your own identity. That's a mistake. You need to do what you know is right."

On Saturday, December 20, 1975, my sister, Berna-
dette, phoned to inform me that you, Dad, had died
that morning at the Bergan Mercy Hospital in Omaha.

The first thing I did after the phone call was to
give thanks to God, and then, Dad, to talk to you.

In this regard I was delightfully surprised to find
that another priest, Father Michael Larkin, had prayed
to his dad the same way I prayed to you. In the Sioux
City, Iowa, *Globe* Father Larkin remarked: "On the
morning that my mother called me several years ago
when I was teaching in Carroll to tell me that my dad
had died, I talked to him while I was shaving, and
while driving to Sioux City. I continue to talk to my
dad eight years later."

Father Larkin went on to say that people who
have known us and loved us while they were with us
on the earth, continue, but in a more perfect way, to
love us and stay close to us after they have gone to
God through the experience we call death.

We can and should talk with those who have died
much in the same way as we did before they died.
They continue to exist, to love us, and to present our
needs before God.

BING CROSBY

The Voice Heard Around the World!

As you know, Bing, the one TV program that pulled on my heart strings more than any other was the two-hour NBC special on the evening of October 28, 1977. It was two weeks after you had died, at the age of 73, from a heart attack, following a round of golf outside Madrid, Spain.

Bob Hope began the program by saying, "I'm sure that Bing is looking down, enjoying this program with us." What a beautiful way to remind us that death does not take our loved ones away from us. "All whom we loved and all who loved us are ever near," so said Cardinal Manning, years ago.

Although you loved life to the full, Bing, you expected the next one to be even more wonderful. You believed that life was planting and growing. Old age was the harvest time. And if life is to be true to nature, after the harvest there could only be another spring.

You, Bing, would agree with Father Anthony Kosnick, professor at St. Mary's Seminary in Orchard Lake, Michigan. "Death is the greatest moment of freedom which opens the transcendent life God extends to all human beings."

Your beautiful wife, Kathryn, was so convinced of this truth that a few hours after learning of your death, she told a news conference in Hillsborough, California, "I can't think of any better way for a golfer who sings for a living to finish the round."

The consoling, beautiful belief in the continued presence of our loved ones was illustrated by your lovely daughter, Mary Frances, the day after you died.

An apprentice actress with the American Conservatory Theater, Mary Frances appeared in a minor role when the troupe's season opened at the Geary Theater in San Francisco with Shakespeare's *Julius Caesar* a day after you died in Spain.

Kathryn, who attended the opening, remarked that both she and Mary Frances were convinced of your continued presence in their lives.

The universal outpouring of love and devotion that followed your death, Bing, gave proof of the power you had to inspire and console others.

In London, mourners stood in the aisles of London's Westminster Cathedral for a Mass said in memory of you, Bing, "a gentle soul who gave such pleasure with unaffected modesty to so many."

In New York, about 3,000 worshipers filled St. Patrick's Cathedral for a Mass in your memory.

Terence Cardinal Cooke described you, Bing, as "a man...of warm presence and outstanding talents...a man loved by millions."

Your great friend and longtime show business partner, Bob Hope, sent the following personal message to Cardinal Cooke's office couched in terms that recalled your love of golf: "He never said an unkind word about anyone whether on life's fairways or in the rough, and that's one scorecard I'd be proud to sign."

Sam J. Taylor summed up your life beautifully when he said that you, Bing, "inspired by example." The gift of a half-century of delightful, wholesome entertainment is a monumental message in itself.

TV-radio critic, Gary Deeb, said of you, that you were "downright breathtaking" in your "versatility as a singer, dramatic actor, comic performer, and genuinely warm personality." You were "a virtuoso at each."

When your wife met the casket at Los Angeles International Airport, she said, "We appreciate all the love we've received from our friends and neighbors. It seemed Bing was everybody's next-door neighbor."

On Tuesday, October 18, 1977, the Mass of the resurrection was said by Father Ellwood Kieser in a chapel in the St. Paul the Apostle's Church in Westwood. Mary Frances led the Responsorial Psalm 23: "The Lord is my shepherd; I shall not want."

The funeral procession followed the freeway to Holy Cross Cemetary and the Crosby family plot where your parents, and first wife, Dixie Lee, are interred.

Your son, Philip, spoke briefly to the press after the burial. "Dad had so much more to give. We all loved him very much. We are proud of the honor paid him—the lighting of the Olympic torch at the Los Angeles Coliseum and the Masses at Westminster Cathedral in London, and St. Patrick's in New York."

You, Bing, made your appearance on planet earth in 1904. When I was a freshman in high school, you were cutting your first record, *Mary Lou*.

In the years that followed, some 850 records racked up astronomical sales of 400 million. By 1934 you were getting 10,000 fan letters a month and there were 85 fan clubs spread throughout the world.

Starting in the '30's you drew millions to their radios. You had your own radio programs on all three networks, most notably on *Kraft Music Hall* with John Scott Trotter. Your theme song was "Where the Blue of the Night Meets the Gold of the Day."

More than any other entertainer during the Depression and World War II you epitomized the highest hopes of Americans. I can still recall the tone of your voice when you sang, "Accentuate the positive, eliminate the negative, latch on to the affirmative, and don't mess with Mr. In-Between!"

It was often said during your heyday in the 1930's and 1940's that at any time, somewhere in the world, the rich baritone of your voice was being heard on a radio, phonograph, or jukebox.

In November of 1939 you signed up with Paramount with your friend, Bob Hope. The result, the famous road pictures: to Singapore, Zanzibar, Morocco, Utopia, Bali, Rio and Hong Kong. This series broke all existing box office records and created a new style of cinema.

You, Bing, made more than 70 films and in each year from 1943 to 1948 you were voted the top money-making star of the movies in an annual poll of theater owners and operators. This made you the all-time champion in the field.

In 1944, you were awarded an Oscar for one of your best-known roles, as a priest in *Going My Way*.

In the movies, as on stage, you seemed always to come on singing happy, upbeat, don't-worry songs that the trouble-weary public loved.

Your love of words, Bing, was evident to all who knew you. You took special delight in letting words flow like magic over your tongue. You had what Bob Hope called, "A soft-spoken way of circumlocution larded with erudite words and foreign phrases that was part of his trademark."

One of the most remarkable aspects of your career, Bing, is that once it waxed big in the early 1930's, it never waned. You aroused unusual affection in your public. You outstripped both General Dwight Eisenhower and President Harry Truman in one popularity poll of the late 1940's. Any one of a variety of casual nicknames—Der Bingle, Old Dad, the Groaner—was enough to identify you in a newspaper headline. In a cartoon your image could be evoked with merely a nonchalant tilted smile, or by one of the pipes or hats you loved.

To you, Bing, I owe a debt of gratitude for all the many songs and the motion pictures you brought into my life. *Sweet Leilani, I'm an Old Cowhand, Pennies from Heaven*, and, above all, *White Christmas*, are never the same for me unless yours is the voice I hear on the record.

Kathryn, your wife, summed up the truth beautifully, "I guess the sound of Bing is woven into the tapestry of many lives."

PRINCESS GRACE
OF MONACO

In 1960, Princess Grace, I had the joy of visiting the Principality of Monaco and was allowed to enter your fairy-like castle perched high on a cliff overlooking the blue waters of the Mediterranean.

When I walked into the elegant and impressive Throne Room, I noticed an inscription in Latin high up on the wall: "The person who says he knows God but does not keep His commandments is not truthful."

By your life, Princess Grace, you proved that you knew God. You also gave confirmation to the words of an unknown poet:

> You can't light a candle
> To show others the way
> Without feeling the warmth
> of that bright little ray.
>
> And you can't give a rose
> All fragrant with dew
> Without part of its fragrance
> Remaining with you.

No one can do anything well in life without a dream, an ideal, a star to follow. It is to your credit, Princess Grace, that you kept untarnished through the years the molten radiant glory of the light from your shining star. You kept the breathlessness, the thrill, the heart's swift running out to meet surprise.

Your life, Princess Grace, filled two chapters: twenty-six years as the daughter of a Philadelphia millionaire who became an Academy Award-winning actress, and twenty-six years as Her Serene Highness of Monaco.

You were born on November 12, 1929, in Philadelphia. Your father, John Brendan Kelly, son of an Irish immigrant, worked his way up from bricklayer to millionaire building contractor and Democratic city chairman in Philadelphia.

As a child you were shy and sickly. You attended the Ravenhill Convent School and Stevens School, both in Germantown. Your mother said that you always possessed a kind of tranquillity and quiet resourcefulness.

As a teenager you studied for two years at the American Academy of Dramatic Arts in New York. You made your professional acting debut in July, 1949, at the Buck's County Playhouse in New Hope, Pennsylvania, where you appeared in *The Torch Bearers*, a comedy written by your uncle, the Pulitzer-Prize-winning playwright, George Kelly.

Your debut on Broadway came later that year in Strindberg's *The Father*, starring Raymond Massey. You appeared frequently in television drama before going to Hollywood in 1951 for a bit part in the film, *Fourteen Hours*.

A year later you emerged as a star with your portrayal of Gary Cooper's Quaker wife in the film classic, *High Noon*.

You won the New York Film Critics Award and an Academy Award as the best actress in 1954 for *The Country Girl*, in which you starred with Bing Crosby. It was during that same year, while making *To Catch a Thief* on the Riviera that you met Prince Rainier.

A week after completing *High Society* you sailed to Monaco for your wedding. You and Prince Rainier were married in an elaborate three-hour ceremony at Monaco's Cathedral of St. Nicholas.

One of the greatest tributes to you, Princess Grace, is that you appeared only in movies to which parents could safely bring their children. You stubbornly adhered to the idea that wickedness was no subject for entertainment. You wanted to conserve the good, the virtuous, and the beautiful way of life.

You never prattled to interviewers, or allowed yourself to be pushed around by producers. You reigned in an era when people expected movies to be entertainment spiced with suspense, romance, and fascinating plots full of intrigue and danger.

One of the most glowing tributes given to you was that from the pen of Mary McGrory of the International Press: "Grace Kelly was blue eyes, fragile blond beauty, white gloves and a slow smile that promised excitement. Her countrymen found her an utterly satisfactory heroine, both on and off the screen. She played romantic roles, she married a prince. There's nobody remotely like her now. Grace Kelly was a great lady. Everyone knew it."

How very true. You, Princess Grace, became part of our lives, a gentle, gracious, luminous friend who helped us down the arches of the years.

When you turned from former movie princess to a real one, Princess Grace, you became a devoted wife, loving mother, and loyal friend of numerous Monaco charities and cultural events.

A friend said of you, "She turned that cold mausoleum of a palace into a warm home."

Actor Jimmy Stewart, your co-star in *Rear Window*, called you "a most accomplished and extremely popular actress. When she assumed the duties of royalty, she did an equally masterful job."

Time and again Hollywood tried to lure you back to the silver screen. You had the wisdom and courage to refuse. You firmly believed that motherhood, home, and family are far more important than any career, no matter how gilded.

Shortly before your death, when a reporter from London's tabloid, *Sunday Mirror*, questioned you on your choice, you replied: "I did enjoy and take pride in my work as an actress, yet I am bemused by suppositions that my life has since somehow been less fulfilling. That certainly is not the case. Rather, the reverse."

The world was shocked in September, 1982, Princess Grace, to learn that you died after suffering a stroke while driving on a hillside near Monte Carlo and tumbling down a ravine in your car.

On September 18th, your funeral was held in the same cathedral in which you were married 26 years previously. The ceremony was led by Archbishop Charles Brandt of Monaco, assisted by an ecumenical group of clergy from Protestant and Orthodox churches, along with a special envoy from Pope John Paul II.

In his eulogy, Archbishop Brandt praised you, saying: "Our Princess was so helpful to others, now she receives the help of our prayers. From now on she will know the most radiant encounter of all."

Newspapers said of you, "The loss of Princess Grace deprives Monaco of a visible symbol of elegance and admirable human qualities. She was an active patron of the arts and of a long list of charitable organizations to whom she lent time and provided publicity."

In Washington, D.C., President Reagan called your death a loss to both your countries. "As an American, Princess Grace brought character and elegance to the performing arts and always found time to make important contributions to her craft."

President Reagan continued: "Princess Grace was deeply loved by the people of Monaco because she was a compassionate and gentle lady who had a deep and abiding affection for her adopted country and people. The principality of Monaco and the world community have suffered a great loss."

Four days after your death, about 1,500 people attended a memorial Mass for you, Princess Grace, at St. Patrick's Cathedral. They heard you praised as a woman who possessed "a special light."

"In his introduction, Cardinal Terence Cooke characterized you as "a great lady of our time who has touched our lives and the lives of millions of people with her God-given talent, her quiet dignity, and most of all, her strong faith and beautiful love."

Face to Face

Now that you have followed my "talking long distance" through the previous chapters of this book, perhaps you say, "O.K., I agree with you. It is wonderful to be able to talk with our dear departed loved ones, but, I feel that something is missing."

Right you are!

In filming a motion picture, after the picture is completed, many long months may go by before the film is shown in theaters across the land. You may have to wait a year to get the audience's reaction.

The first time I became aware of this "time lapse" between filming and showing was in connection with the production of *How the West Was Won*.

A great number of Sioux Indians from Pine Ridge, South Dakota, were taking part in the film. Because of the many magazine articles I had written concerning the Sioux, I was invited to come to the filming location in the Black Hills to write an article on *How the West Was Won*.

Thanks to the kindness of M.G.M. publicity director, Mr. Earl Wingard, that Monday was the most unique in my life. At noon I was invited to have lunch with the stars in their tent, the only place that had a table. All the other people taking part in the film had to eat out in the open, under the blue Dakota sky.

I was placed at the center of the table. To my left was Henry Fonda, on my right was George Pepard, and opposite me was Richard Widmark. I was so captivated by the thrill of talking to these men I can't recall that I ate a thing. Mr. Fonda, in particular, was most kind and thoughtful. After lunch he suggested to me that perhaps I'd like to have a picture taken with him on location.

That afternoon I watched the giant eye of the cinerama camera capture a thrilling encounter on the rim of the forest. It was not until the following year that I had the opportunity to see the cinerama production shown at the Indian Hills theater in Omaha.

The advantage of being on stage, face to face with the audience, according to Johnny Carson, is the thrill of immediate reaction. When you're in front of an audience, you do what you think is funny and get the feedback right away.

Perhaps we may be inclined to take the same attitude towards prayer that is taken in making motion pictures. We put a lot of effort into it, but we never have the thrill of a laughing voice answering our own. We feel that prayer is too much "one way"—from us to our loved ones in our heavenly home. If only we could hear their delightful voices in return.

This, indeed, is the very thing that makes praying a test of our faith. We often do not experience the return of communication we so desire. Listen to the words of agony of a wife who lost her dear husband, after many years of happy, married life.

"In my loneliness my heart cries. I cannot touch his hand. I cannot see him smile. I cannot see his joy. I am trying to feel his presence, but somehow the door has not fully opened to me.

"Our life was so beautiful together. My husband was the doer, the searcher for the beauty and joys of life. When he found them, he shared them with me.

"He was the most appreciative of men. Our life was shared completely. I know that this beautiful person is waiting for me and I am eager to join him. The pain is in the waiting."

The pain of waiting is made bearable if the light of our own resurrection floods our whole lives with its brilliance.

"Do we really have faith," asks Father Charles Gallagher, S.J., "that one day we will rise again, that we as a family will be able to touch each other, hug, hold hands, caress, talk and listen to each other?"

According to Father Gallagher the thought of our own resurrection "should be a brilliant sun that lights our whole existence every day of our lives."

The concluding advice from Father Gallagher is especially fascinating, "Talk about the deceased members of the family—a grandparent, an aunt or uncle. Share how we imagine them now and what we will say to them when we meet them again."

Ruth Goldboss anticipated Father Gallagher's advice by some nine years. In the *Sign* magazine Ruth took us on a tour of heaven via a series of pictures and drawings of outstanding people from various nations and tribes. Underneath each picture was written an imaginary conversation we might well have when we meet these people face to face for the first time.

I liked, especially, the question Ruth tossed to Einstein, "When your parents noted that you were slow to talk, slower to read, and that you failed math in grade school, did they panic and call you an underachiever?"

And the following question to Edison was equally interesting: "My health-food addict friends want to ask if you took extra dosages of Vitamin C to ward off colds in those damp laboratories? If you didn't, knowing what you know now, do you think it is a good idea anyway?"

In concluding this book, my dear reader, may I mention that one of the outstanding joys of heaven I'm looking forward to is the delight of meeting you face to face and visiting with you in person.

About the Author

Take a young boy, turn him loose in the Land of Shining Mountains, alias Montana, and what can you expect?

You may be sure of this—all his life will be filled with visions of beauty, his heart caught high in the branches of the golden aspen on the mountain slope, his dreams pinned tight to that distant star and tangled in the boughs of the tallest pine.

His favorite song will be that of the wind whispering its secrets to the treetops. He will want to return to the mountain thunder, to the silence of the valley. He will hold untarnished through the years the radiant, molten glory of the light from distant stars, white and topaz and misty red. He will keep the breathlessness, the thrill, the heart's swift running-out to meet surprise. He will always keep in mind the words of John Muir, "Climb the mountains and get their tidings. Nature's peace will flow into you as sunshine flows into trees. The winds will blow their own freshness into you, and the storms their energy, while cares will drop away from you like leaves of autumn."

John Scott was born in Omaha, Nebraska, on April 8, 1913. His family moved west the same year.

He grew up in the mile-high, copper-city of Butte, Montana. Fr. Scott attributes his outlook on life to the "mental conditioning" he received from growing up in the Land of the Big Sky, or the Land of the Shining Mountains, as Montana is called. He attributes his love of literature and writing to his mother. She was the one who introduced him to the magic of words, and showed him that books are doors to wide, new worlds.

Fr. Scott began writing in 1938, when he was assigned to Holy Rosary Mission, which is located on the Pine Ridge Sioux Indian Reservation in western South Dakota. He found so many things that were interesting, he thought that people across the nation would like to know about conditions on the Reservation. Thus began a flow of articles for magazines and newspapers that continued to increase with the years.

In 1948, Fr. Scott was sent to Campion High School, Prairie du Chien, Wisconsin, to teach physics. In the autumn of that year he began to write for *The Queen's Work* magazine. For the next fourteen years he had an article on religion or science in practically every issue.

Following the appearance of his articles in *The Queen's Work*, Fr. Scott was asked to edit the science column for *Young Catholic Messenger*. These magazines went into practically every Catholic grade school in the country. His articles on science in *The Queen's Work* were read by the late Father Austin G. Schmidt, S.J., editor of Loyola University Press, Chicago, Illinois. Fr. Schmidt asked Fr. Scott to write a general science textbook. This book, *Adventures in Science,* is the first general science textbook by a Catholic priest anywhere in the world.

Adventures in Science came into the hands of Mr. Emmet J. Culligan, founder of the great soft-water empire that bears his name. Mr. Culligan asked Fr. Scott to write a book on the subject of water. This book, in turn, led to two more books.

To date, Fr. Scott has had 19 books published. His last book, *Beyond Earth,* is a textbook on astronomy for high school students.

In 1959, the Wisconsin Society of Professional Engineers chose Fr. Scott as the outstanding physics teacher in the state of Wisconsin for that year. In April of 1967, the National Catholic Educational Association conferred on him, along with thirty-nine other teachers throughout the nation, the title, "Impact Teacher."

Throughout all his years of teaching, Fr. Scott has been engaged in parish work, especially on weekends. At present, he is the assistant pastor at St. Agnes Church in South Omaha.

Daughters of St. Paul

MASSACHUSETTS
50 St. Paul's Ave., Jamaica Plain, Boston, MA 02130 **617-522-8911.**
172 Tremont Street, Boston, MA 02111 **617-426-5464; 617-426-4230.**

NEW YORK
78 Fort Place, Staten Island, NY 10301 **718-447-5071; 718-447-5086.**
59 East 43rd Street, New York, NY 10017 **212-986-7580.**
625 East 187th Street, Bronx, NY 10458 **212-584-0440.**
525 Main Street, Buffalo, NY 14203 **716-847-6044.**

NEW JERSEY
Hudson Mall Route 440 and Communipaw Ave.,
Jersey City, NJ 07304 **201-433-7740.**

CONNECTICUT
202 Fairfield Ave., Bridgeport, CT 06604 **203-335-9913.**

OHIO
2105 Ontario Street (at Prospect Ave.), Cleveland, OH 44115 **216-621-9427.**
616 Walnut Street, Cincinnati, OH 45202 **513-421-5733.**

PENNSYLVANIA
1719 Chestnut Street, Philadelphia, PA 19103 **215-568-2638; 215-864-0991.**

VIRGINIA
1025 King Street, Alexandria, VA 22314 **703-549-3806.**

SOUTH CAROLINA
243 King Street, Charleston, SC 29401 **803-577-0175.**

FLORIDA
2700 Biscayne Blvd., Miami, FL 33137 **305-573-1618.**

LOUISIANA
4403 Veterans Memorial Blvd. Metairie, LA 70006 **504-887-7631; 504-887-0113.**
423 Main Street, Baton Rouge, LA 70802 **504-336-1504; 504-381-9485.**

MISSOURI
1001 Pine Street (at North 10th), St. Louis, MO 63101 **314-621-0346.**

ILLINOIS
172 North Michigan Ave., Chicago, IL 60601 **312-346-4228; 312-346-3240.**

TEXAS
114 Main Plaza, San Antonio, TX 78205 **512-224-8101.**

CALIFORNIA
1570 Fifth Ave. (at Cedar Street), San Diego, CA 92101 **619-232-1442.**
46 Geary Street, San Francisco, CA 94108 **415-781-5180.**

WASHINGTON
2301 Second Ave. (at Bell), Seattle, WA 98121 **206-441-3300.**

HAWAII
1143 Bishop Street, Honolulu, HI 96813 **808-521-2731.**

ALASKA
750 West 5th Ave., Anchorage, AK 99501 **907-272-8183.**

CANADA
3022 Dufferin Street, Toronto 395, Ontario, Canada.